YOUNG WRITERS

Spellbound

TYNE & WEAR

Edited by Jenny Edwards

First published in Great Britain in 1998 by
POETRY NOW YOUNG WRITERS
1-2 Wainman Road, Woodston,
Peterborough, PE2 7BU
Telephone (01733) 230748

HB ISBN 1 86188 882 1
SB ISBN 1 86188 887 2

FOREWORD

In this, our 5th competition year, we are proud to present *Spellbound Tyne & Wear.* This anthology represents the very best endeavours of the children from this region.

The standard of entries was high, which made the task of editing a difficult one, but nonetheless enjoyable. The variety of subject matter, creativity and imagination never ceases to amaze and is indeed an inspiration to us all.

This year's competition attracted the highest entry ever - over 46,000 from all over the UK, and for the first time included entries from English speaking children living abroad.

Congratulations to all the writers published in *Spellbound Tyne & Wear.* We hope you enjoy reading the poems and that your success will inspire you to continue writing in the future.

CONTENTS

Christopher Robson	76
Daniel Duggan	76
Claire Jamieson	77
Danielle Trotter	77
David Cooper	78
Wesley MacCabe	78
Paul Elliott	79
Craig Paolozzi	79
Zoë Mileson	80
Emma Gray	80
Claire Owens	81
Daniel Filip McCadden	81
Amy Kay	82
Dean Ivers	83
Kathryn McGinley	84
Kirstie Morgan	85
Laura Bainbridge	86
Steven Fallon	87
Amanda Dawson	88
Paul Baptist	88
Wesley Brunskill	89
Stephen Atkinson	90
Jessica Greenhaff	90

Kenton School

Robert Riddell & Craig Spence	91
Kris Abbott	91
Craig Stephen Duggan	92
Lyndsey Walton	92
Kayleigh Chalmers	93
Carley Laskey	94
Stephen Wilkinson	95
Paul Spence	95
Claire Watson	96

Killingworth Middle School
Mark Blanshard	96

Edward Hunter	97
Katie Little	97
Hannah Pearson	98
Jenna Morrison	98
Alexandra Palmer	99
Laura McGill	100
Chris Bowe	100
Sarah Hindmarch	101
Ross Lindsay	102
Allen James Jamieson	102
Sarah Cuthbertson	103
Michael McNally	104
Warren Gunn	104
Andrew Sears	105
Nichola Baker	106
James Walker	106
Katherine Palmer	107
Kelly Hardy	107
Kaylee McCoy	108
Barry Morton	109
Kevin Hodgson	110
Rebecca Bull	111
Phillip Burns	112
Stuart Abbott	112
Nikki Irving	113
Jessica Weightman	113
Dawn Fuller	114
Andrew Yeats	114
Ben Wolf	115
Jill Boardman	116
Diane Douglass	117
John Alexander	117
Adam Mills	118
Darren Smith	118
Iain Kennedy	119
Emma Bayliss	120
Natalie Angelopoulos	121
Ian Black	122

Steven Bolton	190
Lucy McGinley	191
Cheryl Dorosz	191
Shona Richardson	192
Laura Dines	192
Ashya Jacobs	193
David Powell	193
Alison Fish	194
Jamie Gribbin	194
Christopher Harding	195
Craig Fielding	195
Theresa Atkinson	196
Robert Crabtree	197
Malcolm Hurst	197
Danielle Munn	198
Marie Kanu	198
Amber Bone	199
Kelly McKee	200
Samantha Johnson	200
Cheryl Duggan	201
Joseph Jackson	202
Ryan Quinn	202
Victoria Dornan	203
Dawn Foster	203
Eileen Doyle	204
David Goundry	204
Ruth Ashburner	205
Lee McLain	205
Sarah Lambton	206
Jill Clark	206
Amanda Dawson	207
Marie Bryant	208
Nicola Robbins	208
Samantha Johnson	209
Clare Mead	210

St Anne's Mixed High School
Rachel Ford	210

THE POEMS

THE SLOWEST DEATH OF ALL

Rotting eyeball of a leech,
Steal its tongue to stop its speech.
Slice the liver of a dog,
Slowly melt it in a bog.

Steal a liver, steal a lung,
Let these people die when wrung.

Boil the brains of a dragon's head,
Steal a babe from its sleeping bed,
Rip away the legs of the baby,
The cauldron will explode, maybe.

Grind the liver, grind the lung,
Let these people die when wrung.

Peel the skin of a filthy brat,
Take the gizzard of an excruciating rat,
Septic puss from an oozing boil,
Added with blood-soaked soil.

Mince the liver, mince the lung,
Let these people die when wrung.

Take a bird's broken wing,
The dying thing will never sing,
Make up the last of the spell,
When we die we'll go to hell.

Joanne Venus & Jennifer Thompson (12)
Chapel Park Middle School

A SPOOKY SPELL

We call you spooky spirits to arise from the dead,
To show yourself present and come from your bed,

Foaming froth in our cauldron boil,
Whose lives will this sinister spell spoil,

A mutilated liver from a cancerous bat,
And the torn out gooey entrails of a dangerous rat,
Oozing puss of intestines from a putrid frog,
A decomposing corpse, and a decaying dog,

Foaming froth in our cauldron boil,
Whose lives will this sinister spell spoil,

The mouldy tongue of a nagging mam,
The ripped off fingers of a baby in a pram,
Contaminated toes of a smelly foot,
An angry wasp's sting freshly cut,

Foaming froth in our cauldron boil,
Whose lives will this sinister spell spoil,

The revolting remains of a dead man's bladder,
Brain of a slug, and a poisonous adder,
The excruciating lips of polluted camel,
The chopped up insides of a wicked mammal,

Foaming froth in our cauldron boil,
Whose lives will this sinister spell spoil,

The torn out eyeballs of an ugly pig,
A diseased hair from an old woman's wig,
Spiders' legs, and fresh human blood,
This will make things go as they should,

Foaming froth in our cauldron boil,
Whose lives will this sinister spell spoil.

Natalie Grant & Jane Shotton (12)
Chapel Park Middle School

MY FRIEND

You pick me up when I am down.
Wipe away a tear and a frown.
A light shines with a single smile.
You're a friend who's caring, sharing
and loyal.
You saw when I was in the wrong.
I was sad and lonely and you
made me so strong.
You gave me the confidence that
I never had.
Sweetened things up when
they got bad.
And just to say thank you,
I'll give all this back to you.
As friendship always works both ways
So give it to someone,
It always repays.

Helen Hajek (11)
Chapel Park Middle School

LE SORTILEGE

Bloody sharks' teeth and a bat's cancerous wing,
Mixed all together with a jellyfish sting.
The skull of a baby drowned at first birth,
Added to the cauldron with some polluted surf.

Slice them, and dice them and grind them to dust,
Mash them, and smash them, scream if you must.

Oozing puss from a putrid frog,
Stir up the mixture with a bone from a dog.
Acid rain and a bag of drugs,
Add to the mixture with some villainous thugs.

Slice them, and dice them and grind them to dust,
Mash them, and smash them, scream if you must.

Ten lit cigarettes and a barrel of beer,
Put into the mixture with a leg from a deer.
A pint of blood and a cat's mashed up brain,
Add to the pot with a lion's mane.

Slice them, and dice them and grind them to dust,
Mash them, and smash them, scream if you must.

Add some fire from the burning depths of Hell,
Spice up the mixture with a really vile smell.
Eye of newt and toe of dog,
And the entrails of a festering frog.

Slice them, and dice them and grind them to dust,
Mash them, and smash them, scream if you must.

With a wasp's sting, and a cobra's bite,
Call up these Demons with terrible might.

Andrew Brown (12) & Scott Mason (13)
Chapel Park Middle School

FRIENDSHIP IS FOREVER

Friendship is caring for one another.
Feeling helpful and happy.
Knowing that she will always be there.
Thinking she will be there to talk to.
Happy when we are having fun.
Sharing our thoughts and secrets.
Wanting to know her all of my life.
Hating when we have a fight.
Never to break up.
Friendship is trusting each other.

Amy Knighting (11)
Chapel Park Middle School

FRIENDSHIP IS . . .

Friendship is when I play with him.
Feeling happy when he's there.
Knowing he will always be my friend.
Thinking what he's thinking when I see him.
Happy when he's happy.
Sharing sweets when he's got none.
Wanting to play with him.
Hating to be apart.
Never betraying him.
Friendship is between two people.
                              Friends.

Mark Roche (11)
Chapel Park Middle School

I'LL ALWAYS BE YOUR FRIEND

Whenever you're down or feeling low, I'll be there,
I'll never go.
Whenever you're alone and can't see for tears,
I'll come round to cure your fears.
I've been your friend throughout the years,
and when you need me I'll always be there.
You can rest on me when you feel weak,
I'll be in your dreams while you sleep.
When you're left all alone, I'll come round to say 'Hello'
When you're down and start to cry,
I'll come round to make you smile.
When I'm away on holiday you can rely on me
to phone each day.
When you're in trouble and need a hand,
I'll stand up for you in every way I can.
As long as you know I'll always be there.
I'll be happy and a good friend.
I'll stay with you through the bad times and good,
I'll be loyal like I should.
I can keep a secret I would not tell,
because I am your very best friend.

Kay Lister (11)
Chapel Park Middle School

FRIENDSHIP IS FOREVER

Friendship is forever and always.
Feeling good inside, being happy.
Knowing that someone is there for you.
Thinking someone cares for you.
Happy when someone is around you.
Sharing thoughts and feelings.
Wanting to be a good friend.
Hating when you fight.
Never being horrible to your friend.
Friendship is trust.

Katherine Pritchard (12)
Chapel Park Middle School

MY JOURNEY TO SCHOOL

On my way to school,
All traffic lights are red.
It is an unwritten rule,
It does not need to be said.
The jams are at their worst,
Impatient drivers get furious.
The roads are about to burst,
The thought of it makes me curious.
For I always think this fate,
Is planned to make me late.
About other drivers I do not care,
They're still standing stationary there.
I'm late for registration,
This is such a frustration.
This is definitely not *fair!*

Shayma Saleh (12)
Dame Allan's Girls' School

SPELLBOUND

I woke up in the morning,
And went to check the mail,
There was one letter on the doormat.
I opened it carefully and read,
As I stared,
I was star struck,
I was spellbound.

'I've won!' I cried!
'One million pounds!'
Mother came and had a look.
Her mouth dropped open,
As she stared,
She was star struck,
She was spellbound.

We sat motionless on the settee,
It was as if we were paralysed.
I looked at the phone number,
We looked at it perplexed,
As we stared,
We were star struck,
We were spellbound.

I dialled the number carefully,
Somebody answered,
It was dad!
'April fools,' he said.
As we stared at each other,
We were star struck,
We were spellbound.

Scarlett Moore (13)
Dame Allan's Girls' School

SPELLBOUND

After nine months of waiting he's finally here:
His eyes, his ears, his perfect little nails,
That angelic little smile no one can match.
I'm spellbound, quite spellbound, by my new baby brother.

When you go to hold him,
He grabs you with chubby, pink fingers and squeezes quite hard,
And then with the strength of a giant he tugs at your hair.
I'm spellbound, quite spellbound, by my new baby brother.

And then he cries;
He howls and yells with all his might, but then along comes *mum,*
After a quick feed all is well.
I'm spellbound, quite spellbound, by my new baby brother.

It's three o'clock, and time for his afternoon nap.
His bright observant eyes follow the brightly coloured mobile,
Slowly his tiny little eyes close and he drifts off to sleep.
I'm spellbound, quite spellbound, by my new baby brother.

He wakes refreshed and ready to go,
He gurgles cheerfully to attract attention,
Obeying his command I pick him up
His nappy is *wet!*
Oh well, maybe I'm not so spellbound after all.

Helen Hines (13)
Dame Allan's Girls' School

SPELLBOUND

Perhaps I was bemused,
Maybe even charmed,
But I'm sure I was bewitched.
I could have been captivated,
And possibly enthralled -
Entranced? Absolutely!
I was certainly hooked,
A little enraptured as well;
But possessed?
I could have been transfixed;
I was positively under a spell!
Riveted? - I don't know.
For certain I was hypnotised!
And just a touch fascinated,
But I'm not quite sure about mesmerised.
But spellbound? - definitely!

Emma Cruickshank (14)
Dame Allan's Girls' School

SPELLBOUND

The stars mesmerise me,
Encrusted in the light,
I am bewitched by this spell,
The splendour I see this night.

Like jewels they all gleam,
And take my breath away,
Sapphires, rubies, pearls,
How I wish they were here to stay.

I can't help but be captivated,
Flabbergasted - I am rapt,
Gripped I am star struck,
I can't move, I feel so trapped.

Transfixed I can only stare,
Hypnotised I stand,
Never in my life,
Have I seen the sky so grand.

Andrea Nirsimloo (13)
Dame Allan's Girls' School

SPELLBOUND

On Friday night I was unable to sleep,
So I gazed out the window, onto the street.
I saw out the corner of my eye,
A flash of orange swept the sky.
I turned and saw to my surprise,
The sun was about to come and rise.
Reds, oranges, yellows and blue,
All of these colours, some of them new!
The sun came up, bit by bit,
Even more of the sky it lit.
And as it rose higher,
All I could do was admire.
I lay there, silently spellbound,
At all this loveliness that I'd found.
So tomorrow morn, when all is still
I'll be up and watching at the window-sill.

Rachel Atkinson (13)
Dame Allan's Girls' School

SPELLBOUND
(A tribute to Diana, Princess of Wales)

Spellbound by your beauty,
Enraptured by your grace,
Startled by your
Ever glowing face.

Charmed by your charity work,
Your love,
Your gentle, graceful, compassionate
Love for all.

Hooked on you.
A star-struck designer's dream,
Entranced the public eye.
Under a spell as you passed by.

Gripped by despair,
Divorce and bulimia,
You fascinated us so much,
In energy, love and pain.

Mesmerised we remember you,
Ever beautiful, glowing, young,
We were dazzled by you,
Yet we persecuted you.

Now all we see is your image,
Captured on camera,
All your feelings,
Generosity, love, compassion,
Only occasionally hate,
If only we could be like you.

Now for the final obsessed glimpse,
It's ironic if you just pause,
Diana, the Hunter, Queen of Hearts,
Became Diana the Hunted.

Hannah Lee (13)
Dame Allan's Girls' School

THE VOICE

All eyes looked up,
Every mouth dropped down.
The room turned silent,
Except for one sound:
That crystal clear voice,
Ringing out, swirling round.
Enchanting our ears,
Intriguing our minds.
A voice without source,
So noble and kind.
Whilst a rainbow of colours,
Before my eyes danced.
I stood as if hypnotised,
Completely entranced.
Paralysed, mesmerised,
Totally enraptured.
Heart, soul and body,
So willingly captured.
Then the voice started fading,
A transient spell?
A dream or reality?
I really can't tell.

Katie Brodie (13)
Dame Allan's Girls' School

SPELLBOUND

The moonlight is shining in the thick bleak wood,
It's full of mysterious things:
The owls are hooting,
The bats are flying,
Over glittery fairy rings.

The sky is dark but the stars shine bright,
The moon is shining, too.
The witches cast their spells over the silvery dew.
A mystical house is in the woods,
Inside it lives a witch,
Who mixes her potions in a pot,
That looks as black as pitch.

In it she puts a spider's wing,
A beetle's leg, or two.
She stirs and stirs the cauldron up until it's a thick black stew.

Her ebony eyes glisten in the dark,
She never gives a glance.
To see the giant who lives nearby,
Watch her, as if in a trance.

She dances round until the dawn,
She really is obsessed.
The transfixed giant cannot move: he really is possessed.

Around she goes until the dawn,
Then back to her home she goes.
It is now the early morn,
As well the giant knows.
Although he cannot move a limb,
He was so hypnotised.
He doesn't know until this day,
Why he was mesmerised.

Farzana Malik (13)
Dame Allan's Girls' School

SPELLBOUND

I saw him,
I heard him,
He was landing on the roof:
His footsteps as soft
As a reindeer's hoof.

Then down the chimney he did fall,
And landed in the decorated hall.
He was as wet as snow, and as cold as ice,
But that didn't stop him,
Not for a trice.

I watched enthralled,
As he walked to the tree,
And started unloading his sack.
The dog was amazed,
The cat was bewitched,
But I remained bemused.

I pretended to be asleep,
But I just had to peep.
Then he saw me, flabbergasted and shocked.
He laughed through his belly,
And had to lean on my telly,
Though I could not see why it was funny.

I remained in a trance,
Till his reindeer did prance
From my roof that night,
And out of sight.

Claire Urwin (13)
Dame Allan's Girls' School

THE VISITOR

The hall felt different, somewhat spooky,
Like an icy ledge on a frozen gate.
A smoky shape from around a corner appeared,
Like a gathering of dust breaking free.
As the starlight shone onto the intruder,
No shadow was cast onto the wall behind.
The audience, astounded sat back amazed,
As this visitor unfolded its hazy limbs.
Their mouths open, faces pale and eyes like black holes,
The audience stared with breathless excitement,
Never experiencing a moment as unreal as this.
Only dreaming of events of this nature,
As the gloomy figure drifted centre stage.
It picked up a hat and walking cane,
And with the aid of music from an invisible orchestra,
It waltzed rhythmically in mid-air,
Like a cloud over a dark black sky,
Being blown around by the wind.
The dancing dust suddenly came to a halt.
And bowed to a mesmerised audience.
The audience clapped and cheered loudly,
But eyes were still fixed onto the anonymous visitor.
In a hypnotic state like mechanical robots,
The audience clapped monotonously in a paralysed state.
The bewitching character bowed again and all of a sudden
The noise of thunder rumbled from above.
The lights flashed on and the enchanter disappeared,
And the play carried on as before.
But this was a night never to be forgotten,
For it was his finest performance of all times.

Natalie Dick (13)
Dame Allan's Girls' School

BEWITCHED

Long day at school, tiring, boring, meaningless.
Trudging home, heavy school bag, blisters.
Suddenly, a small kitten with wire round its neck,
Bend down to help it, lovingly, caringly, kindly,
Remove wire from its neck, choking wire, writhing wire.
Kitten thankful, comfortable, breathing, relief.
Suddenly, kitten falls, in pain, no, mesmerised, paralysed,
Calling, drawing me to it.
Kitten smiling?
Jerking, cursed, bewitched, captured!
Under a spell, reaching, beckoning!
Me, fear, frightened, scared, what is happening?
Is it dying?
Is it teasing?
Is it crying?
Is it dead?
No movement, eyes transfixed, unblinking, dead.
Body, still, cold, lifeless, dead.
Why can't I move?
Fixed to the spot!
Panic, then tranquillity, the kitten walks to a white light,
Beauty, enthralled, so majestic, pretty, pure,
Is this white light heaven?
the kitten disappears, I run, desperately trying to follow.
White light smaller,
No!
White light gone.
I've seen heaven?

Jane Harding (13)
Dame Allan's Girls' School

SPELLBOUND

As I stood on the summit of the mountain,
All I could see were trees.
The hillsides were spread before me,
In a million shades of green.

I was fascinated in Switzerland,
Enthralled and entranced,
By high rocky mountains, thick woods,
Deep blue lakes and clear ice-cold streams.

Eagles, storks and herons,
Dragonflies of green, blue and red,
Pink and grey loach silkily swimming,
In the cold, dark, smooth river.

Old half-timbered, stone buildings and farms,
Steep roofs, arches, and metal-covered west walls,
To protect from wind and rain.
Colourful steeples and towers on churches,
Red, blue and green tiles shining in the sunlight.

Each place I visited was better than the last,
Each more entrancing and exciting.
I was totally and utterly, most obviously
                              Spellbound!

Rebecca Evans (13)
Dame Allan's Girls' School

SPELLBOUND

Staring out of the window,
Watching things go by,
My mouth is gaping open,
There are circles in my eyes.

I'm completely paralysed -
There's nothing else to say,
Except that I'm entranced,
A spell made me this way.

But I cannot move, I cannot speak,
I'm fully transfixed to the floor,
My knees are wobbly - my body's weak,
And I can't take any more!

This ghostly charm inside me
Is driving me round the bend,
I wish I wasn't so obsessed,
What will I tell my friend?

Oh, it's over, it's finished,
So *that's* what made me this way,
I think I have just witnessed
The best ever fireworks display!

Laura Kadleck (13)
Dame Allan's Girls' School

THE DRESSAGE ARENA

You will see it all day in a field eating grass;
Often grubby or shabby with no pretences of class.
Look at the rider away from the ring,
And you'll see nothing special, just a chap doing his thing.
So for most of the time, this is what it will be,
Until they are ready for the public to see.
Then the whole scene's transformed as the dressage begins,
What a sight to behold! Both as bright as new pins.
They perform with such beauty, such charm and such grace,
With the equerry and rider so exact with their pace.
It no longer remains just a man on a horse,
But artistic perfection through the whole of the course.
Every move is poetic - not a movement untried,
So emotive their gestures, so majestic their ride.
The precision is there to be seen all around,
And I sit watch spectacle, completely spellbound.
As the show nears its end and the two come to rest,
It is clear that we've witnessed a taste of the best.
And throughout this short time when the spell had been cast,
We're transformed from mere mortals through a state unsurpassed.
But thereafter when returned to mere human and horse,
It is hard to believe that they were such a force.
And I wait for the next time when my spell will again,
Bind me over, swishing tail, flying mane.

Rachel Sainthouse (13)
Dame Allan's Girls' School

SPELLBOUND

Magic wizards with wizarduzz charms,
Wicked witches who always alarm.
Shooting stars way, way up high,
Star struck, splendour, outer space. Why?

Spellbound.
Bewitched, entranced, enchanted, transfixed.
Way out of this world. To be enraptured, enriched.
To be whizzed from this earth, transported, possessed.
To be hypnotised and mesmerised and under a spell,
To travel on a broomstick. Visit heaven and hell.

I wonder with wonder at the sight.
It's spinning, it's twisting, it's twirling tonight.
Can it be magic? I'm under a spell,
I'm spellbound, I'm star struck and now unwell!

Laura Hewison (13)
Dame Allan's Girls' School

THE BULLY

The scream in my stomach,
The nerves, when will they start?
Will it be at registration,
Or will they leave it until break?
If I don't say anything will they keep quiet?
Why don't the like me?

Who will be the bully today?
They come in all shapes and sizes.
Will it be someone unknown?
Please don't ask me a question,
I want to be anonymous.

If I answer right I am a swot,
If I get it wrong then I am thick, an idiot.
If I don't answer and walk away they follow me.
If I retaliate it's what they want.

Whose fault is it, the bully or the bullied?
I should do this, I should do that,
If I was only like this,
Taller, better at football, witty,
Then maybe they would like me,
Or maybe not?

But then I think,
It's them that should be pitied, not me.
I have so much.
To act as they do they must have nothing.
Perhaps they have been bullied too.
Desperately unhappy to take it out on me.
I shall stand tall and strong and do my best.
After all, I only have one life.
Why waste it because of them?

Andrew Dickinson (12)
Dame Allan's Boys' School

THE BIG APPLE TREE

As I wake up, a morning sun peeps through my window,
Which then makes me think of the big apple tree.
As I draw my curtains, I peer over the neighbour's fence
And what a beautiful sight.
A glowing tree which is framed with golden apples.
Then my mind goes back to spring and I think of what it once was.
A small brittle shoot supported by a beam.
I then think what progress this tree has made.
But most of the time I think, oh what a beautiful thing!

Kirsty McEachin (12)
Emmanuel College

A TIRING DAY

Rocks that we wanted to sit on
On the walk we listened to all the sounds
The trees were blowing in the wind
Hills were very tiring to walk up
But not tiring to walk down
Under some rocks and trees there was nature
Rothbury is a very peaceful place
Yet the day was very exciting.

Amanda Shaw (11)
Emmanuel College

THE FOUR SEASONS

Spring's here, spring's here,
This is the start of a new year,
The grass is green, the sky is blue,
Young lambs and birds, lives are new.

Summer's here, summer's here,
The hottest season of the year,
Wining and dining, in the sun shining,
Everyone's having fun.

Autumn's here, autumn's here,
The nights grow cold and long,
The leaves turn crimson, gold and red,
And fall off the trees because they are dead.

Winter's here, winter's here,
This is the end of another year,
Snowflakes fall around your feet,
Christmas pudding for us to eat.

Catherine Nye (12)
Emmanuel College

FIREWORKS

Fireworks, fireworks you give us a fright,
But you fly up and brighten up the night,
You dash, you dance, you whoosh, you woo,
But everybody comes to watch you.
When you go high you make a loud sound,
Then your flakes fall to the ground.
People come to watch you, more and more,
To watch you go up and fall to the floor.
You go up and light up the stars,
Some people come walking, others in their cars.
You look beautiful, you take over the sky,
I hope I'll see you again bye bye!
Some smell smoky, some smell clean,
Some look gentle, some look mean.
When you go off, dogs bark,
They run into a corner and hide in the dark.
If you go off far too soon,
You might make a noise and wake up the moon.

Benjamin Willey (11)
Emmanuel College

GOING FAST

Walking past the window, trying not to look,
I know all about it, I read it in my book.
I've read about the paintwork, its shiny chrome and leather,
So smooth and cool with perfect lines and style.

Just think, running free along country roads,
And brushing past the cows in the fields.
Feeling the wind against my face,
It's all just a dream, but makes my heart race.

Rudy Foster (11)
Emmanuel College

THE SEASONS!

Summer, summer is a time to laugh,
Seeing children playing football on the path.
When the sun shines the weather turns really fine,
Summer, summer is a wonderful time.

Autumn, autumn when the leaves start to fall,
Children stop playing with their ball.
Sometimes in autumn it starts to rain,
That's when autumn turns a pain!

Winter, winter is really cold,
This is when the jumpers are getting sold.
Everything covered in a sheet of white,
Winter, winter is a wonderful sight.

Spring, spring is the time of year,
When the weather starts to get fair.
All the newborn can't even bite,
Spring, spring is a wonderful sight.

David Baggaley (11)
Emmanuel College

HOW SUMMER GOES

Summer goes like the
clicking of a switch,
the ringing of a bell.

The bright colour of the sun
fades in the background
as the gloomy winter
takes its hold.

The school children moan and groan
as they wonder where
their holidays have flown.
They think of the good times
and the bad times.

But I just want to know
why the summer had to
end!

Alan Bell (12)
Emmanuel College

THE ROSE

The rose,
Stands there in all its glory,
Pink and green,
With thorns as sharp as a blade,
But pretty as a rainbow,
Cold and wet from the morning dew,
Still the rose stands there,
Alone and peaceful,
Its petals, soft as the world's best silks,
Soon It Will Die.

Rachael Sharp (14)
Emmanuel College

MY FIRST DAY AT SCHOOL

I was so very nervous at my first day at school
Was I going to get my head, flushed down the loo
But the teachers helped and guided me
So when it came to tea
I could eat what I liked and to me it was free

> But when it came to lessons
> My fingers went all cold
> I was told to count up to ten
> But only managed four

My favourite part of school
Is when we all go home
I sit on my favourite stool
And watch some old cartoons

> I enjoyed my first day at school
> Except for one small thing
> When I woke up
> It had all just been a dream.

Adam Borlace (11)
Emmanuel College

THE SEA

The shiny waves upon the sea,
Fill the fishermen with glee.
All kinds of fish, with colourful gills,
All cooked up in a very hot dish.

Upon the beach the children are splashing,
And on the rocks the waves are clashing.
The fisherman breathes in ready to shout,
'Come over here, I've caught a trout!'

The lifeguard screams, 'Someone's in trouble!'
Watch him run down the beach of rubble.
The sun goes down, the sea is black,
Don't worry sea, tomorrow we'll be back.

Peter Dias (11)
Emmanuel College

STARTING EMMANUEL

When I started the Emmanuel I thought
I would be overcome by homework,
But I have managed to survive,
I survive by work.
I survive by day.
I survive the school.
I survive OK.

I have been there one month so far.
One month ago I was on my way to school.
I was thinking,
Got my books.
Got my pencil case.
Got my brain in.
Got my PE kit just in case.

In the future I will be sitting tests.
In the hall with Mr McQuoid.
Standing at the front saying,
'There will be no talking.
There are forty-five minutes left.
There will be no copying.
There are no missing questions.'

Paul Forster (11)
Emmanuel College

DARK

I dread the time when I go to bed,
For when I wake up I might be dead.
You might say 'Why should that be?'
Well come in closer and listen to me.

The hand under my bed, could punch up my head.
The monsters behind the door, could crawl along the floor.
The spiders on the ceiling, give me a shivery feeling.
The wolf that sneaks up quietly, would bite me and he'd munch me.
The ghost that comes through the dusty old vent,
Would scare me till I made camp in a tent.
My action men would start a war, and would not give up till
I made peace on the floor.
But all that doesn't matter, for in the end,
I know my mum's just round the bend.

Faye Hession (11)
Emmanuel College

COW

Cows are not supposed to fly,
And so, if you should see,
A spotted cow go flying by,
Above a paw paw tree,
In a pork pie hat with a green umbrella,
Then run right down the road
And tell a lady selling sarsaparilla,
Lemon soda and vanilla,
So she can come here and tell me!

Peter Armstrong (12)
Emmanuel College

THE RIVER

River, river flowing along
every day you sing your song.
Coming down from mountains high
then vanishing back into the sky.

It's far to the blue sea
that seems where you want to be.
Never stopping for a rest
putting your power to the test.

But before you reach the sea
you get sucked in through pipes just for me.
We drink you, splash you, all day long
but still you play the trickling song.

Andrew Harris (11)
Emmanuel College

WINTER

I love winter when it's cold outside,
I can snuggle up in bed,
And hear the wind roar against the window,
I feel warm and cosy.

I love winter, playing in the snow,
On my sledge, having snowball fights,
And building snowmen, some fantastic sights!
It's fun outside.

I hate winter, the nights are long and dark,
It's freezing cold and the car will never start,
It's cold at school, your muscles freeze,
It's far too cold in winter!

Michelle Wilson (11)
Emmanuel College

I HAD . . .

I had a baby caterpillar.
It was a little wriggly thing.
He had a bicycle with a bell.
He liked to make it ring.

I had a baby bumble bee.
It had a pointy tail.
It liked to fly around all day,
And ended up in jail.

I had a baby pussy cat.
It had a ginger tail.
It thought it was a puppy dog,
And collected in the mail.

I had a baby budgie.
It had a yellow bill.
It liked to fly around all day,
And reckoned it was ill.

I had a baby hamster.
It liked to twitch its nose.
It liked to run around all day,
And get squirted with the hose.

I had a baby brother.
A little annoying thing.
He liked to play with the telephone,
And make it go ring ring.

I had a baby alien.
It liked to eat jam tarts.
It was weird and strange,
But I loved him with my heart.

Joanne Nicholson (11)
Emmanuel College

THE BULLY

Every night at 4 pm,
I would wait in horror for the bully men.
They'd take my belongings, empty my bag,
For the bully leader is as strong as a stag.
And you're wondering why nobody stopped them,
From doing this crime over and over again.
For it wasn't just anywhere they gave me a thump,
It was in the school dinner dump.
I would go into school the very next day,
And all the children straight away,
Would be asking me why,
How on earth did you get that black eye?
And I would reply,
The bullies came along.
They're as big as King Kong!

Jillian Bennett (12)
Emmanuel College

AUTUMN

Brown and gold leaves fall from the trees,
As I walk outside to be greeted by the crisp autumn breeze.
My footsteps crunch on my new golden path,
My thoughts are ahead of me dreaming of a nice hot bath.
The children outside are running around and playing,
Their enjoyment goes without saying.
Bonfires burning, a blaze of light,
Red flickering flames an amazing sight.
All I can say is that it is too much for me,
I'm going in now for a hot cup of tea.

Laura Newby (11)
Emmanuel College

ALL HALLOWS EVE

The night drew near,
The darkness fell,
The air was misty,
It had a rotten smell.

The candles flickered and waved in the air,
The shadows moved here and there,
The leaves were rustling,
I felt really scared,
So I hid in the garden,
The garden shed.

There were webs in the corners,
Spiders in my hair,
But I didn't mind,
I didn't really care?

The door creaked open,
I looked in despair,
What should I do?
So I shouted 'Who's there?'

It was a scarecrow with a stick,
With a lump on the end,
As it stepped into the light,
I could see the lump on the stick,
Was my father's head.

He banged the stick off the shed,
So I picked up the rake,
And I knocked off *his* head.

The head began to scream,
As it rolled on the floor,
So I ripped it up . . .
The screaming was no more.

Hallowe'en, Hallowe'en,
You will feel scared,
But don't forget to run,
Or you'll end up dead.

Jonathan Rogerson (12)
Emmanuel College

THUNDER AND LIGHTNING

Strips of light fill the sky,
great big bangs way up high.

People frightened everywhere,
children hiding here and there.

Fork lightning is worst of all,
great big raindrops also fall.

You count how far away they are,
I would be crazy to be in my car.

If you knew what they can do,
you'd be scared in case it happened to you.

The worst thing that they have done,
is to strike a man's house just for fun.

There's three kinds of lightning and they're all bad,
sometimes they've made people go mad.

The sky lights up electric blue,
cats and dogs are frightened too.

Thunder warns you of the strike,
then suddenly the sky is all alight.

Michelle McMahon (11)
Emmanuel College

AUTUMN

In the autumn the leaves fall off the trees,
The weather changes,
And everything seems to die away.
The leaves are brown and on the ground,
The trees just look so bare,
And everything seems to have died away.
The weather is windy and rainy,
It seems all cloudy and dull,
And everything seems to be dying away.
The animals are hibernating,
And won't reappear till spring,
And everything seems to be fading away,
And they won't appear till spring.

Lindsey Wardle (11)
Emmanuel College

MAGIC

Magic, Magic everywhere,
Magic, Magic in the air.
If you meet it face to face,
Run, run, run to a hiding place.
Magic can be evil or good,
But if I had it I think I would:
Turn my fish into a cat,
Take a bunny out of a hat.
I would put my brother in a cage,
Before he went off in a great big rage.
Magic isn't a piece of cake,
It's as hard and sharp as a garden rake.
So please, please, please, be aware,
If you meet Magic you're in for a scare!

Rachel Nichol (11)
Emmanuel College

THE LAST DAYS OF PRIMARY SCHOOL

I went into school for the last day,
I didn't think it would ever happen,
But the time has just flown away,
My netball teacher bought us a gift,
The nice thought just gave me a lift.
I went into the yard, everyone was sad,
Even I didn't think it was going to be that bad.
The afternoon came,
Nothing would ever feel the same.
There was a party in the hall,
You could hear people crying through the wall.
People felt sick,
Then it went so quick.
The time had just left us,
and then the noise of the school bus.
Everyone said their goodbyes,
But the yells and screams filled my eyes.
I had got my last school report,
and I looked back and thought
of all the things that school had taught.

Amy-Marie Williams (11)
Emmanuel College

THE NIGHT OWL

At night when all the lights are out,
The owl goes flying round about.
From tree to tree he dives and swoops,
Then you will hear his nightly hoots.
But when he sees the light of day
To his rest he flies away,
To sleep and dream of his nightly scheme.

Jennifer Cliff (11)
Emmanuel College

A SUMMER'S DAY

The clouds float by in the pale blue sky,
As if some great being from above,
Had blown the dust away from some old book.
The crimson sun gently shines on my face and reflects off my eyes.
It makes pretty patterns on the surface of the passing brook.

The tall trees sway in the gentle breeze.
An emerald leaf softly floats down,
From the heavens onto luscious grass.
Birds above sing as if they were in love,
As they gently glide past.

I dip my hand into the brook,
And move my hand to feel cool running water,
Running between my fingers.

The gentle crackling sound of running water,
Reminds me of some fantasy I have.
The smell of freshly cut grass lingers around my head.

I stretch out on the luscious grass under the tall tree,
Listening to the gently running brook.
I drift into another dimension.

Hollie Walker (12)
Emmanuel College

AUTUMN DAYS

When the leaves turn crisp, gold and brown,
The sound of rustling in the town,
The wind howling around the empty streets,
Chipping off wood on the old park seats,
From the window all you can see,
Is a tapping on the window off an old oak tree.

The dew on a misty morning leaves a trail upon the grass,
And the mist that covers the hills soon begins to pass.
The rich smell of aromas of freshness in the air,
It's here and gone, no one knows that it's been there.
The swallows leave for a warm destination,
Egypt is their proposed location.

The frost on the windows, cars and roads,
The sound of skidding tyres from the lorries, which carry the
heavy loads.
The early morning traffic delays,
Danger in driving due to the haze.
The autumn days don't last forever,
When winter comes so does the cold weather.

Adele Leach (12)
Emmanuel College

THAT MANGY MUTT

That dog keeps scratching at the door,
Does it want to be out?
Not now, it wants more!
Go and feed it,
Let it out.
I feel just about ready,
To kick, scream and shout!

Whose is it anyway?
Who brought it in?
We've got lots of dog food!
I'll open a tin.
Okay we can keep it,
It's ours anyway.
I thought someone brought it in,
From a dustbin.

We bought it from a pet shop,
It scratched at my foot,
It gave me a yucky bath,
Oh that mangy mutt.
Someone just let it out,
Or take it for a walk,
I must be the only one,
Who can hear himself talk.

I suppose I'll get up,
For one stupid pup,
And turn off the TV,
For that mangy mutt.
Now that he's happy,
And we're in the park,
I think I'll let him off his leash
To go for a lark.

Daniel Metcalf (11)
Emmanuel College

MY DOG!

My dog's a Dalmatian.
Oh what a creation!
He's the best in the nation.
My dog's a Dalmatian.

My dog's name is Spot.
He once slept in my cot!
So I smacked his bot!
My dog's name is Spot.

He won't harm a soul.
A bird or a mole,
Or even a foal.
He won't harm a soul.

He jumps up at me,
When I make his tea.
He really loves me,
When I make his tea.

When I take him for a walk,
I will always talk,
To the other dog owners,
As we pass them by.

And now Spot's asleep,
He won't stir or creep.
He won't even weep,
Now Spot is asleep.

Matthew Siddle (11)
Emmanuel College

CROCODILE

He's so cute and nice I told my mam
But would she let me keep him?
No!
I told her about how he was an orphan
and he had no teeth
But would she let me keep him?
No!
Please! No!

His skin is the colour of green grass
But would she let me keep him?
No!
I told her about how he didn't eat much
and kept his bedroom very tidy
But would she let me keep him?
No!
Please! No!

Then I told her if we didn't take him
He would end up being a rich woman's bag and shoes
Would she let me keep him?
Please! *Yes!*

Rachel Jobson (11)
Emmanuel College

MY MAM

My mam can be a right old grouch,
Shoving us and bossing us about.
Saying 'Your room's not tidy,' or 'Look at your hair,'
It's like she follows us everywhere.

My dad likes mum really a lot.
They laugh and joke around.
And mum's always there to pick me up,
Whenever I fall down.

And when I think about it,
She's kind and cares a lot,
About her loving family.
We are all she's got.

Katrina Rowan (11)
Emmanuel College

THE COLT

The large brown eyes stare at me, longing for more food.
I lift my hand, holding it flat.
I let him take the apple wedge from my palm.
While he eats, I put the bridle on him.
I lead him to the mounting box. I climb the box and
Pull myself onto his back.
With the slightest pressure of my legs he breaks into a trot.
I lean further forward and wheel him around on his hind legs.
We charge as one, flowing around and speeding at the gate.
Just as we're about to collide with the fence,
He launches himself over, landing gracefully on the other side.
Once again I lean further forward, adding more pressure
While moving my legs into position.
The sunset comes as we charge at the next fence.
As we clear this fence we are free of fields and meadows.
The stars shine bright as we splash through the river,
Crash through the trees and bash through the flower beds.
Too late I realise we've gone too far.
He crashes on and then stops, nearly throwing me off his back.
The black colt nuzzles beside the white filly.
I know next year there'll be a special foal,
The foal of the black colt Midnight and the white filly Moondance.

Joseph Douglas (12)
Emmanuel College

SCHOOL

A buzzer sounds.
It fills the air with much awaited news.
Chairs scrape,
Doors bang,
Laughing children stream out the doors.
At last everything is silent inside.
Worried teachers sit down,
Sorting out last night's work,
And having a cup of coffee to calm them.
Teachers in the staff room chatter and laze:
Until, one by one they finally depart.
Once the last is gone the silence returns.

A few early risers the next day,
Sauntering quietly around the yard.
The buzzer goes,
Lessons begin,
Another day of work has begun.
Homework is given,
Books are collected or given.
And, before someone realises,
The buzzer sounds its mournful tone,
Home time!
Pupils stream out the doors,
Another day gone by.

Heather Shield (12)
Emmanuel College

A TIRING WALK

A raincoat was not necessary on the walk.

The cow-pat was not a very nice scene, or smell.
It was a very tiring walk.
Rocks were there to sit on when you were tired.
It was also very exciting.
Not very easy to climb up the hills.
Going on the walk gave me cramp.

We never got to walk along the wall itself.
And I had sore feet when I got back.
Long walking is exciting.
Kicking stones was not allowed.

Philip Cornes (11)
Emmanuel College

MY FOOTBALL SONNET

Football is really great,
I play it all the time;
I always play it with my mate,
When I'm not making up a rhyme.
It's a game played by eleven men,
Well, a team in fact,
That play again, and again,
Almost as if they've made a pact.
When a team scores a goal,
They laugh and play,
And joke and fool,
Because they are so happy and gay,
To play the game that's called football,
A game enjoyed by almost all.

Arran Cockburn (13)
Emmanuel College

LOVE

From a window I watch my love so fair,
As he nears I feel my heart skip a beat,
Then into the arms of my love who cares,
But with a warmth that holds me: this love so sweet.

With a passion that sweeps me off my feet,
I feel dizzy beyond my wildest dreams,
In this world was never a love so deep,
My knight in white armour is all he seems.

Bringing flowers and gifts given with love,
These words of love he so tenderly speaks,
Holding me close like the gentlest of doves,
I feel the breath of my love touch my cheek.

All my life I will love no other,
Our days will be spent loving one another.

Victoria Wilson (14)
Emmanuel College

MY GRANDDAUGHTER

My housework is done and everything's shining,
Now I need half an hour's reclining.
There's a knock at the door and somebody small,
Is waiting to tumble right into my hall.
Two laughing eyes, an infectious grin,
'Come on grandma let me in.'

'Have you got any biscuits today?'
'None at all darling,' I hasten to say.
Crumbs on the floor and beakers of pop!
Excuse me a moment whilst I get the mop!

Jennifer Hurst (12)
Emmanuel College

THE RAINFOREST

The darkness falls on what's left of the rainforest,
Like a black blanket of mystery.
The stars sparkle as if diamonds
Had been thrust into the sky.
And the moon shines like a beaming torch
Through the darkness.

The cries of the monkeys echo
Throughout the rainforest,
And the crunch of the panda eating bamboo
Can be heard in the distance.

As the beautiful waterfall cuts its way
Through the rocky mountains,
Holding secrets that nobody knows,
Birds flock from tree to tree,
The Jaguar settles down for the night with her cubs,
Surrounded by old banana leaves and twisted vines.

Tree lizards crawl up the ancient trees,
Knocking dead leaves of all colours
Twisting and turning to the ground.

As the everlasting sun sets upon the horizon,
The whole rainforest settles down for the night,
Not knowing what challenges the rainforest
Will bring to them in the ongoing fight for survival.

Julie Kimber (13)
Emmanuel College

MIND OF MAN

In the mind of man lurks a darkness of insane reason,
A gallery of endless questions.
A landscape of unexplained answers.

Such complexity is the way of chaos,
And the reality of Nature.
And the mark of order is simplicity,
The dream of Man, which can never be.

Why seek cruel truth?
To leave the semi-comfort of the unknown lie.
What pulls us all to this wise youth?
Is it the authority of Justice, that causes the subconscious pangs
                                          of our consciences?

If all answers do is to create questions,
Why do we ask, why do we seek the unseekable?
And if all questions are unanswered truths,
Why do we endeavour to ask them, do answers even exist?

And what twisted realms of madness could create,
Love, and Hate.
Is it we, do we create out of some need,
If so do we treat it as a toy, and so we destroy?

Is there a need for prejudice, if not why create?
A crude judgement, may save.
But who would make black to slave?
Mislike him not for his complexion, but for his wrongs.

Logic has no meaning,
Yet is, everything and nothing.
Perhaps the easiest way to live would be to abandon questions,
                                          answers, love and hates,
But I would dismiss this for would we be Human?

And when all the greatest minds have debated and stated,
And all the beliefs have argued and destroyed themselves, who
                                        will be left to reason,
A sea of silent discussion or a desert of chaos, what will be?

Dhruv Sookhoo (13)
Emmanuel College

IS IT FAIR?

Cutting down the rainforests,
Just to make a chair.
Using up the fossil fuels.
Stop to think,
Is it fair?

Oh so many dirty cars,
Choking up the air.
Choking up the atmosphere.
Stop to think,
Is it fair?

Dropping litter to the ground.
Notice the people stop and stare.
Just to save yourself the bother,
Stop and think,
Is it fair?

Why cut down the animals' homes,
For a sheet of paper?
Which you will scribble on and tear.
Stop to think,
Is it fair?

Karen Lapsley (13)
Emmanuel College

SUNSET

The bright shining sun shines through the day,
From dusk till dawn, while the children play.
When the sun and the land can say they've met,
The beautiful *sunset.*

The glow of the sun that brings colours gay,
At a sight like this what can you say?
There is no argument, no need to bet,
About the beauty of the *sunset.*

As it dies into the night,
No more colours, no more light,
Everyone saying 'What a sight!'
The dazzling *sunset.*

David Partington (13)
Emmanuel College

CHILD

Children are a piece of gold,
Something that you must always hold,
In your heart they will stay,
Right until your dying day.

Right from the moment when they are born,
Till the day dawns early morn,
They will say 'I love this child'
Oh so gentle, oh so mild.

You don't know how much you love them till they're gone,
Then you know they're the only one,
Something so precious something so mild,
Then you know it is a child.

Danielle Hall (12)
Emmanuel College

MARTIN THE WARRIOR

Fur and freedom cry out aloud,
Your enemies will die at the sound,
Follow the warrior with the sword,
Come let's defeat the enemy horde.

Fight back with all your might,
Don't let them get out of your sight,
Remember they had hit you with whips and canes,
Remember they drove you mentally insane.

Throw the javelins,
Sling the stones,
Make sure you break their bones,
'Hurry moles and dig those holes,'
Victory is there but exactly where?

Badgers, squirrels, shrews, and mice,
Kill the weasels in a trice,
Let the warrior attack the stoat,
That leads the enemy horde.

The warrior mouse fights the veteran stoat,
To gain revenge and take back his father's sword,
That he lost to the Tyrant stoat,
'Come on Martin kill him proud,
With the weapon that you wield.'

We won the battle but friends were lost,
'Martin don't leave you made us win,'
But he walked south,
To live in peace at Redwall Abbey.

Christopher Bell (12)
Emmanuel College

THE STORM OF ANNIHILATION

Thunder rumbles in the night sky,
Lightning sets ablaze the darkened night sky.
The sea thrust about the tiny boat,
Engulfed in the large catastrophic waves.
Like a rock hurled by an angry mob,
The boat is tossed about.
Many of the crew try to abandon ship,
Before the boat is smashed.
Before they have a chance to enter the water,
Death with his crooked claws,
Snatches the boat and all aboard forever,
Claiming them for his own.

Years after the unfortunate end of the boat,
It is sighted by some fishermen.
They sail in closer for a better look,
But little do they know who looks upon them.
It is our old enemy Death,
Who never abandons his watch,
Always ready to claim more lives.

Sundeep Singh (13)
Emmanuel College

VENUS FLY-TRAP

I have a plant sitting on my window-sill,
It rivals with the local spiders.
All flies are terrified of it,
Yet not one actually knows what it is.
One by one they cautiously go,
But not one returns.

My plant spares no lives but doesn't hunt,
It just stays still . . . Until . . .
The hairs on its mouth-shaped leaves tingle,
Then it comes to life and very slowly closes,
Another life gone.

Tim Hayward (12)
Emmanuel College

HOW LONG IS A MINUTE?

When I fancy a game on the computer, I'll say,
'Dad, would you like to play?'
He'll reply, 'Yes in a minute'
But it doesn't quite happen that way.

When I'm looking for something I'll call,
'Mum have you seen my football?'
She'll reply 'I'll help you look in a minute,
I'm just finishing this phone call.'

When I've washed the dishes I'll cry,
'Sis, it's your turn to dry.'
She'll shout 'I'll be there in a minute.'
But I know it's a lie.

I thought a minute was 60 seconds long,
But it seems that I was very wrong,
For it seems to last for hours, in my home.
So exactly *how long is a minute?*

. . . 'David, are you getting up for school?'

'Yes, in a minute!'

David McDermott (14)
Emmanuel College

THE LITTLE PRINCE

Once upon a time in a far away land,
There was a Prince who wanted a tan.
His skin was white, as pale as could be,
'Cos the weather was cold (he lived by the sea).

So one day he called the *Royal Adviser,*
Instead of his dad; he was no wiser.
He asked him nicely, 'What should I do?'
The adviser replied, 'It's up to you.'

The Prince got angry, he wanted him dead,
So he shouted his loudest, *'Off with his head!'*
The adviser pleaded down on his knees,
So the Prince said smugly, 'Come, follow me.'

He led him to a corner where no one could hear,
And whispered quietly into his ear . . .
'I'm going to Spain to get a tan,
And you can't stop me, you mean, old man.'

Hannah Ward (12)
Emmanuel College

MAGIC

It's magical and mystical,
It's totally bizarre!
It will make you wander past,
The biggest, brightest star!

The wizards and the witches,
Make the world a different place,
With magic hats and magic cats,
And moons with a face.

Silver star dust, and a wand,
Hand in hand we go along,
Through a dreamy restless sleep,
Who knows what creature we will meet.

Crooked grins and gale-force winds,
The magic word, *'Whiz'*
But do you really know,
What magic really is?

Emma Bray (12)
Emmanuel College

DIANA

Our Princess' love will live forever,
Blossoming like a rose inside our hearts,
While love that she made filled the world over,
She died like the sun ready to depart.

Unlike a candle her soul forever,
Glowing and blossoming inside each son,
Giving us love that brought us together,
Sharing the delight of the work she'd done.

Gone up to heaven gone to take her place,
To where the media cannot touch her,
Gone now has that honest lady of grace,
She's gone to heaven not even a stir.

How we all loved our fairy tale Princess,
She'll stay in our hearts 'The People's Princess'.

Jayne Batey (13)
Emmanuel College

CHRISTMAS TIME

Christmas time is full of joy,
Lots of gifts for girl and boy.
Shops are full up to the brim,
With decorations, Christmas trim.
Barbie dolls and Action Men,
Crying dolls and Mr Men.

Now it's nearly Christmas Eve,
Baubles hanging on the trees.
Santa Claus will soon be here.
Everyone, give out a cheer.
Carrots and a drop of sherry,
No wonder he is very merry!

Christmas day is old and gone,
New Year's day is still to come.
Next year's 1998,
Let's just hope it will be great!

Heather Nickerson (12)
Emmanuel College

WHY?

Why was I crying?
Why did I cry?
What was I waving . . .
Waving goodbye?
Why was I freezing?
Why did I freeze?
What was making that chilly breeze?
Why was it snowing?
Why did it snow?
This is for you and me to know.

Danielle Stephen (12)
Emmanuel College

THE MAN OVER THE ROAD

Over the road is a grumpy old man,
With thick white hair and not much tan.
He walks his dog all day and night,
With a fag in his mouth, he'll give you a fright!

When the man walks by he smells of smoke,
It makes me think he'll start to choke.
His dark brown dog is very old,
At times it must feel freezing cold.

At half past eight on every night,
He goes down the street and out of sight.
Walking past the bushes and trees,
His jacket blows in the gentle breeze.

Matthew Silversides (12)
Emmanuel College

DEATH AND DARKNESS

In the beginning there was darkness
At the end there is death
What you start you must finish
Darkness kills light
Death kills
These two are precious and sweet
Ending pain and suffering
With an icy grip
Run in to the sorrow of darkness
Give in to the arms of death.

Kaye McCluskey (13)
Emmanuel College

RUINED MILES

The valley bordered by Hadrian's Wall,
Beside the hills, great and small.
See the ghostly soldiers fight,
Or is it shadows in the night?

Imagine what tales these hills could tell,
Scenes of battle, where soldiers fell.
Marching for hours, day by day,
Then reaching a mile-house, a place to stay.

Stretching its way from Solway to Tyne,
Its stones were laid in a long, straight line.
Eighty miles was its length,
It took six years of men with strength.

This huge barrier was fifteen feet tall,
Its ten foot width made it a mighty wall.
This second century wall still lies,
In ruins, still for miles and miles.

All year round the tourists come,
Whatever the weather, rain, snow or sun.
On slippy ground, some stumble and fall,
Along Emperor Hadrian's hand-made wall.

Ruth Nordmann (13)
Emmanuel College

THE FLOWER

Pollen is enclosed by a tight little bud,
As the day crawls near and morn' returns to night.
The bud explodes like a firework in space,
Unveiling the petals with the flower segments inside.

Kate Armstrong (13)
Emmanuel College

AUTUMN

Autumn comes round once a year,
Crisp brown leaves floating in the air,
A blanket they form on the ground,
Before the north wind comes,
And throws them around.

In the park under the trees,
Down on our bended knees,
Searching for conkers big or small,
It doesn't really matter - we collect them all.

As daylight gets shorter,
And the dark nights draw in,
The farmers are out,
Doing their deeds,
Harvesting the fields,
For the winter feeds.

Craig Lawson (12)
Emmanuel College

CLOUDS

Flying high, flying low,
Floating where they want to go.
White and fluffy,
Dark and light,
Thunder and lightning,
Oh so bright.
Formations forming in my mind,
Dancing, weaving, running blind.
To see them form to see them run,
I sit and watch,
And have such fun.

Gemma Johnson (12)
Emmanuel College

AUTUMN

Autumn is the time for crisp brown leaves,
Drifting down, from the trees.
Children running, searching for conkers,
They're so ambitious, people think they're bonkers.
They're climbing up trees, and on the walls,
Chucking up sticks and huge footballs.
A big, brown conker hits the ground,
Towards the conker the children bound.
No one stops, no one stalls,
More conkers hit the ground like big, brown balls.
Walking and running on the leaves so crisp,
It's like standing on salt 'n' vinegar crisps.
The sun is shining through the clouds,
Just looking at it makes you feel so proud.
Looking at the litter cluttering the ground,
The people who dropped it I'd like to pound.
The trees go dark, it's getting late,
Next thing you know you're at the garden gate.

Daniel Case (12)
Emmanuel College

WE'LL MEET AGAIN

A soft sound whispers in my ear,
For once, I wish that you were near,
I wish that your voice I could hear,
You're special to me, you are so dear.

I sit alone all cold at night,
I bear the pain with all my might,
How could you do this to me?
I lie alone and think of thee.

And as the years go by and by,
I'll sit and grieve and wonder why,
It did not turn out for the best,
So you go east, and I'll go west.

But while I write this poem for you,
I know our love was always true,
But wait! Is that your voice I hear?
Perhaps we'll meet again some year.

Andrew Robinson (13)
Emmanuel College

HALLOWE'EN

H   owling, hungry wolves haunt
A   ll of the villages where
L   aughing children play, 'trick or treat!'
L   ongingly the wolves gaze
O   ut of nearby bushes or shadows
W   hen they really want their own treat to
E   at. Screaming children carried away.
      Carried, from their homes and play.
E   aten alive and then when old wolfy
      has had enough he slyly slides to a place
N   earby to await his next victim.

Children beware on Hallowe'en
Children take care on Hallowe'en
If you don't look carefully round each bend
The wolf will get you in the end!

Kate McCready (12)
Emmanuel College

DIANA

Diana, was she a Princess?
She was to all of us.
She did so much for so many,
But would have loved to do more.

If only she'd had the chance,
To live her life longer.
She could have changed this world,
More than anyone has done.

Princes William and Harry,
My heart goes out to you both.
If only you could have had,
Your mum around you more.

I know she'll always be,
In the hearts of both of you.
Not to have your mum around,
Must be very hard to bear.

You've got your family by your side,
They are here on Earth.
Your mum will always be watching you,
From heaven up above.

Lisa-Marie Berry (14)
Emmanuel College

THE FRIENDLY MONSTER

He's a big yellow monster,
With a grin on his face,
He has green polka dots
And boots with a lace.

He's friendly with children,
When they all come out to play,
They play lots of games,
For the whole of the day.

Kathryn Bagnall (12)
Emmanuel College

DEATH

Death, the object of fear,
when you are old he draws so near.
Our lives are like ribbons entwined,
till death cuts us short and soon they unwind.
Time is cruel but not for death, if not for a second or eternity,
death always outlives you and me.
Whatever age, we are within his grasp,
his voice so cold, a seething rasp.
He flees to shadows and evil chasms filled with mourning.
He takes no prisoners (hardly so) for where his feet tread,
none may go.
His coldness, sternness, piercing eyes, could even waken the soul
of him who dies.
And when you take your final breath, you then will know
the fear of death.
We cannot comprehend his presence, a being spanning time itself,
a giant taking no form.
But neither can we feel his sorrow, a monotonous, painful task is his.
His heartfelt lamentations rent the air, as he mourns for the evil
he has become like daggers piercing the moonlit sky.
A sepulchral pit, his living place, where none can gaze upon his
disfigured face.
Tormented, misunderstood, it's all too much he has no help to lend.
Now all he can hope for is his bitter-sweet end.

Ben Tormey (12)
Emmanuel College

THE SEA

I look into the deep blue sea
And think about my family and me
My mam, my dad and my sister too
We've looked at the sea just like you
The sea is many colours - purple, blue and green
You pick out all the colours, and think of
Something you've seen
Maybe it's some chocolate, velvety as can be
Or it could be a big, blue ship floating through the sea
Standing on the shore, your imagination running wild
You think about your life
When you were a child.

Karen Hull (13)
Emmanuel College

CHRISTMAS

Snowflakes begin to fall from the sky,
Glistening and sparkling as they go by.
They cover, like a blanket, the ground with white,
And it gives off a glow like a light.
The lights shine brightly on the tree,
Heavily laden with presents for you and me.
It's Christmas again and the mood's so jolly,
The walls are covered with berried holly.
The best part of all would have to be,
Christmas morning with presents for me.
But it will be back next year,
And will probably be even better.

Lindsay Dews (12)
Emmanuel College

WHY I LIKE SKATEBOARDING

I love to ride my skateboard,
And every chance I get,
I scoot along the pavement,
It's faster when it's wet.

I jump the kerb,
I pull a skid,
And even though I try,
I can't jump over dustbins,
Because they're far too high!

I always wear my helmet,
'Cos if you hit the deck,
You get a crack across the pelmet,
Or even break your neck.

Chris Stephenson (13)
Emmanuel College

THE CANADIAN BUTTERFLY

The Canadian butterfly,
Bright and beautiful,
She knows when the day is true
Off she goes blowing in the wind,
She knows this is her final journey.
Destination Mexico, to mate and to die.
Tired and exhausted she arrives
With the other butterflies,
Falling like leaves from a tree.
She dies happy, knowing she has created life,
Her fragile body will nourish the soil
and Mother Nature will take care of her.

Louise Stott (13)
Emmanuel College

MIDSUMMER NIGHT SKY

When darkness puts the day to rest,
And the heavens belong to the moon.
This is the time that she likes best -
Her stars will be out soon.

The midnight sky belongs to her,
And she glorifies in his worth.
Gently she smiles her secret smile,
As she gazes down on Earth.

Andromeda, Pegasus, Cetus the whale,
Majestically shine in the night.
The southern fish suddenly twitches her tail,
And the dark sky explodes with her light.

Altair the eagle spreads his wings,
And the triangle sparkles with gladness.
Polaris appears and all the stars sing,
For this glorious midsummer madness.

Sagittarius, Capricorn, Libra,
Appear silently, twinkling their light.
Hercules sits at the centre,
Holding court for his moon queen tonight.

Now moonbeams with love and contentment,
Her stars are all playing their part.
To rid Earth of all hate and resentment,
The wish dearest of all to her heart.

Sarah Tulip (13)
Emmanuel College

MY GRANDMA

My grandma's getting older,
I think she's 64.
I don't care what her age is,
I'll love her even more.

She's always bright and chirpy,
She's always on the phone.
Her friends are quite uncountable,
She's never all alone.

Shopping is quite fun with her,
She buys me lots of gifts.
I don't know what to do with them,
They come in oh so swift!

My grandad and her are quite different,
They do their own little things.
My grandad's into computers,
While my grandma likes to sing.

She always dresses smartly,
She never looks a mess.
She either wears a blouse and skirt,
Or a smart long dress.

Overall she's quite unbeatable,
She could never be replaced.
The things she wears and buys,
In life, she has good taste.

Cheryl Hall (13)
Emmanuel College

THE CAT

The cat is very intelligent.
It has amazing reflexes,
And the most incredibly beautiful eyes.
The razor sharp claws,
Glint in the sun.
It soars through the air,
Flying downwards and landing perfectly,
Always on its feet.
The soft paws pad lightly on the ground.
The short, sleek coat is kept in
Pristine condition by its owner.
The tail flicks lightly,
And the gentle purring and miaow,
Is such a beautiful sound.
The cat is so intelligent.
It plays at night with others of its kind.
At morning it dozes in the sun,
Resting its tired body.
What an easy life.

Melanie Simblet (12)
Emmanuel College

A ROLLERCOASTER SONNET

Twisting and turning,
Looping and spinning,
My stomach is churning,
I'll try to keep grinning.

You sit in your seat,
And they strap you in tight,
You think it's a treat,
But you'll find it's a fright.

You rise up to the skies,
And leave the Earth behind,
Don't shut your eyes,
Just hope gravity is kind.

Then you plummet to the ground,
And wish it were a merry-go-round.

Kris Dunn (13)
Emmanuel College

A Day On The Hills

Hills and beautiful scenery-

T rees were everywhere.
R ivers were deep and blue.
E astern moss smelt nice.
E normous mountains.
S heep were in the fields.

Things you took -

L unch to eat.
U mbrellas in case it rained.
N apkins for lunch.
C oats for cold weather.
H ats for your head.

How you felt -

T ired a lot.
I nterested in the view.
R efreshed after lunch.
E xhausted by the end of the day.
D rained of all energy.

David Young (11)
Emmanuel College

PLANE POEM

On my ceiling hanging down,
There are planes all around,
Jump-jets like the GR7,
And bombers like the F111.

Tiny trainers and planes that fill up the sky,
Old rusty biplanes which hardly fly,
Tornado, fighting Falcon plus Foxbat,
Fishbed, Flanker and Tomcat.

Planes swooping down on prey,
Planes on my ceiling night and day,
On my ceiling hanging down,
There are planes all around.

Sebastian Lambert (13)
Emmanuel College

HARVEST

Harvest is the time of year,
When everybody knows,
The benefit of reaping,
What the farmer sows.

Early in the springtime,
The tractor ploughs the fields,
The seeds are planted in the ground,
In the hope of generous yields.

Because the farmers gathered the crops,
To make us all grow strong,
We take in nutrition and use it well,
To help us all year long.

Helen Todd (12)
Emmanuel College

A WALK IN A WOOD

Entering a wood,
Led by a winding path.
Tall trees looming over,
I nervously walk past.

Cricks and cracks,
From everywhere.
I try to block them out,
I think they're coming closer.
They make me want to shout.

I try to walk a bit faster,
My pace is close to jog.
It's getting rather late,
I can see the coming fog.

I'm getting quite frightened,
I cannot find the end.
I'm getting rather worried,
I wish I had a friend.

At last I see a hazy light,
Glistening through the gloom.
I step outside into the night,
And see the shining moon.

Reyhan Dhuny (12)
Emmanuel College

The Shadows

As I walk the dark shadows let me see no path.
Nothing apart from the leaves of the tall oaken trees,
That catch every ray of light.
I clutch my coat tightly around me,
For only a second to see one patch of light
Would fill me with joy.
I hear whispers in the leaves of the trees.
I picture a room.
In the corner is a warm flickering fire.
As I open my eyes the image fades away.
I am once again trapped in the loneliness.
It brings me a sudden urge to run.
To escape the emptiness,
To escape the fear,
To escape the darkness, and the cold,
And the desperation.
My heart pounds.
My eyes dart about searching for a route to escape!
To see once again the sun.
I stop. The trees open out into a small clearing.
What a wonderful place.
Delicate blue flowers grow amongst golden grass.
The rays of the shining sun shower sweet flowers.
A dusty path leads out of the forest.
It was clear to see now, not hidden by blackness,
And I am safe!

Victoria Harris (12)
Emmanuel College

IT'S SUMMER!

It's summer, it's summer!
Have fun in the summer.
Call all of your friends,
And have fun in the sun,
Till the fun ends.

The warm, bright sun,
The gentle breeze,
And the smell of blossoms,
Growing from trees.

It's summer, it's summer!
Have fun in the summer.
Call all of your friends,
And have fun in the sun,
Till the fun ends.

The dew on the grass,
The sound of the birds,
Cheeping and chirping,
Some things sound better,
Some things sound worse.

It's summer, it's summer!
Have fun in the summer.
Call all of your friends,
And have fun in the sun,
Till the fun ends!

It's summer again!

Lianne Roberts (13)
Emmanuel College

WINTER'S COMING NEARER

It is becoming very dark now,
You can't be on the go.
Winter's coming nearer,
Blustery winds and snow.
Crispy brown and yellow leaves, fall upon the ground,
Every time you step on them, they make a crunching sound.
There are no kids playing in the park,
Because after all it is far too dark.

Outside the snow has been falling all night long,
It's time to get up now and put our winter warmers on.
Building snowmen can be such fun,
For children and almost anyone.
Snowflakes fall one by one,
Falling lightly gliding down.
The robins around us looking for food,
I wonder if we can help them out.
For that is what winter is all about.

Sarah Swanston (12)
Emmanuel College

MONTY

Monty is a cat in black velvet.
His fur is like silk.
He eats lots of cat food,
And drinks lots of milk.

He plays around me,
And claws my little sister.
He jumps onto my mother,
Then once he nearly missed her.

He curls into a ball at night,
And falls sound asleep,
And if a burglar was to come,
He wouldn't make a peep.

He wakes up in the morning,
And stretches out his claws.
He comes and cuddles into me,
And ice cold are his paws.

Andrew Whittaker (12)
Emmanuel College

SCHOOL

It's my first day at Emmanuel today,
I don't know what to do or say.
Dad takes me in the car,
Down the road, it's not too far.
In the morning we have a break,
I have a drink and a bit of cake.
At twelve o'clock we have our lunch,
We all sit down in a bunch.
At four school's at an end,
Outside I see my friend.
Karen's sitting in the car,
To take me home it's not too far.
Now it's homework time for me,
After that I'll have some tea.
Now it's close to bed,
To rest my weary head.

Adam Ainley (12)
Emmanuel College

AUTUMN LEAVES

Autumn leaves are falling from the trees.
The leaves are yellow, red and brown.
The leaves are blowing along with the breeze.
The leaves are falling, falling down.

There is wind, rain and even snow.
The days are short and very cold.
The nights are long and colder, though.
The children are happy, excited and bold.

The season will soon be ending.
The snow is on its way.
'Cause Christmas will soon be coming,
And that will be a happy day.

Christopher Robson (12)
Emmanuel College

HADRIAN'S WALL

H aving fun is important,
A s everything is perfect.
D ays always sunny.
R ain hardly ever comes.
I t's got all kinds of flowers,
A nd lots of trees.
N ew insects are always everywhere.
S warms of bees in the trees.

W aters are as clear as a mirror,
A nd there are lots of lily pads.
L eisure is pleasure at Hadrian's Wall.
L ovely sights for you to view.

Daniel Duggan (11)
Emmanuel College

COLOURS

White -	White as the clouds in the sky,
	As white as cotton buds.
Yellow -	Yellow as the sun,
	With its big hot rays.
Black -	Black is the colour of darkness,
	In the night.
Blue -	Blue is the sky on a sunny day,
	On a warm sunny day.
Red -	Red is the colour of wallpaper,
	In Victorian times.
Green -	Green is the grass,
	Swaying in the breeze.
Pink -	Pink is the sunset,
	On a lovely warm night.
Gold -	Gold is the ring,
	That you wear on your finger.

Claire Jamieson (12)
Emmanuel College

THE WALL

As we walked across the wall,
It did not seem long at all.
The wall was packed with stones so high,
I almost believed they could touch the sky.
As my friends ran on ahead,
Lauren fell and banged her head.
As I wandered on I slowly thought,
Of all the men that had fought.
The wall was packed with stones so high,
I thought they definitely could touch the sky.

Danielle Trotter (11)
Emmanuel College

HADRIAN'S WALL

H is for happiness when you start the walk
A is for anger when you stand in mud
D is for dizziness if you're afraid of heights
R is for red hot boiling sun
I is for inconvenience on the way there
A is for apples in a packed lunch
N is for no roads for miles
S is for sweet baby lambs

W is for walking for miles
A raincoat wasn't necessary
L is for long day
L is for lunch not far away.

David Cooper (11)
Emmanuel College

HADRIAN'S WALL

H ills as big as mountains.
A dults to guide the way.
D anger on the dusty roads.
R oads as long as string!
I went to Hadrian's Wall as well.
N obody was sick or ill.
S ights to see.

W alls with holes for sheep to get out and in.
A ll the children were feeling glum.
L azy sheep in the hills.
L azy sheep in the hills.

Wesley MacCabe (12)
Emmanuel College

MR FLUMP

Mr Flump is such a grump,
He always calls me a fat lump!
I always hate it when he calls me that,
So in my head I call him a fat rat!
Every day he takes us on walks,
He even makes us do daily talks!
He always tells us what to talk about,
Even though we are in doubt!
Every day at 3.30,
He lets my pals and friends go free!
He tells me off each and every day!
He tells me to put the stools away!
I really hate all school days,
But most of all I hate Mondays!
I really hate Mondays because we have RE,
And after that we have PE.

Paul Elliott (12)
Emmanuel College

A GOOD DAY AT ROTHBURY

R ocks to sit on when you're tired,
O ak trees all around,
T   rees to look at while you're walking,
H ills to sit on for your lunch,
B ig and little rocks all around,
U sing big sticks to climb up high hills,
R ivers to see and ducks as well,
Y oghurts for when you're hungry.

Craig Paolozzi (11)
Emmanuel College

BUTTERFLIES

B eautiful are butterflies, so graceful they fly
U nannounced they flutter into your life
T ouching them makes you forget everything else
T rying to imagine what they are thinking of.
E ver flying in every direction. Trying to confuse you.
R ings on their bodies and soft hair.
F luttering in the pale blue sky
L anding on brightly coloured flowers
   and smiling at you in a shy way.
I magine being a butterfly. Not having a care in the world.
E yes on their wings. Seem to watch your every move.
S hining happiness and putting a smile on everybody's face.

Zoë Mileson (12)
Emmanuel College

LIFE

Life itself holds many mysteries,
So I've been told.
We start as babies in nappies,
Then we mature and grow old.
What I can't work out,
Is what life's meant to mean.
Time and time again, I shout,
'What's meant to happen in between?
Still there is no answer,
To direct me in the right way.
Nobody will ever point a finger,
So I'll have to walk astray.
Until I reach the right road,
I'll have to slot life together like cardboard.

Emma Gray (13)
Emmanuel College

SCHOOL

As the children wait for the teacher to come,
They all decide to have some fun.
They jump up onto the desks,
And strangle people by their necks.
Some of the children enjoy to fight,
They even dangle from the light.
They shout and laugh and scream and giggle,
And get out their paper and begin to scribble.
Then not much later the teacher will come,
And that is the end of all their fun.
Off the lights,
Off the desks,
No more strangling by the necks.
Then they all sit down to learn some more,
Even though it is a bore.

Claire Owens (12)
Emmanuel College

ARE YOU A WIZARD?

There was an old man who lived in a castle,
He wore a blue hat with a golden tassel.
Never did he step outside of his door,
Not even when challenged by the law.
Old wizard Marvin had such a long beard,
That all who saw him thought he was weird.
He often made such pungent spells,
That even his raven couldn't abide the smells.
Marvin ended up dying at two hundred and two,
If you meddle with spells this could be you!

Daniel Filip McCadden (12)
Emmanuel College

HALLOWE'EN

Hallowe'en is here,
The 31st of October.
We all set out,
With our costumes on,
To 'Trick or treat',
On people's doors.
Apples bobbing,
A full moon up there,
Witches flying,
In the sky.
Awooooo,
Goes the werewolf.
Spiders crawling,
Everywhere,
Pumpkins glowing,
With an evil face.
Black cats,
Purring by.
Nightmares,
In the minds,
Of young children,
Trying to sleep.
Midnight comes,
Tick, tick, tick, tick, tick,
One minute past midnight,
Hallowe'en is over.

Amy Kay (12)
Emmanuel College

COFFEE

As you can see he's ready to go,
With a record set by Nescafe Gold Blend Boomer.
It'll take some beating at twenty point nought six secs,
But, we all know he's got what it takes.
There he is, getting set . . .
And he's off!
He swerves round the dog,
But no! The kettle has no water in!
He hurdles the dog, grabs the kettle, turns . . .
Oh no! He has hit the dog - repeat hit the dog!
This is costing him vital seconds!
But he's up and the kettle is full.
One thing I can always say about this lad, he's a fighter.
He is now opening the fridge and . . . Oh!
The milk's in mam's shopping bag!
He pulls the milk from mam's shopping bag lightning fast,
And pours . . . He slams down the milk,
And lunges for the sugar with the time at fourteen point six seconds.
He has got to work harder!
The sugar is in and he leaps for the co . . .
No coffee!
What a tragedy!
But yes! There's still hope! There's a few dregs in the bottom.
He enters the few grains that remain and skips over the dog.
There it is . . . The Nescafe Gold Blend . . . He enters the coffee and . . .
Relax . . . Oh no! He must tidy up or it's an automatic . . .
Disqualification! They think it's all over . . . 'Click'
It is now.
That valiant effort doesn't even affect the score table.
So that's all from me, it's over to you Des.

Dean Ivers (12)
Emmanuel College

AT OUR SCHOOL

At our school there's so much fun,
The teachers say 'Now please don't run.'
Our friends who always try to please,
Detention or not they're down on their knees.
There's also fun with prefects around,
They sometimes say 'Don't make a sound.'
And at our school we do not rest,
We always, always do our best.

At our school we're very proud,
We never, ever shout out loud.
We have our lessons, they are great,
We are never, ever late.
Our parents are proud and feel so great,
When we walk through the best school gates.
It's good to be a pupil there,
'Cause schools like ours are very rare.

At our school we all look smart,
To those less fortunate we give our heart.
We raise money in any way,
Whatever we get we give away.
To foreign countries who have nothing new,
But lots of wars all year through.
We wish for peace where people mourn,
And all the people who are forlorn.

At our school we are a team,
We're always nice and always gleam.
You've probably noticed who we are,
'Emmanuel College' the best by far.

Kathryn McGinley (12)
Emmanuel College

SEASONS

Summer

Summer is the time for a nice big blue sky.
People are going on vacation.
The children are playing happily in the park.
The beaches are full of people sitting on the glossy sand.

Spring

Newborn lambs are learning to walk,
Flowers are blossoming.
The days are getting longer.
Easter is near.
Chocolate! Chocolate! Chocolate!
That's all people can think of.

Winter

The ground is white with snow.
People are sledging down hills.
Parents are rushing about for Christmas.
Excitement is the main thing.

Autumn

The leaves are falling off the trees.
Animals are going into hibernation.
The nights are getting shorter.
It's time to start getting wrapped up.

Kirstie Morgan (12)
Emmanuel College

THE FOUR SEASONS

Spring

Daffodils and crocuses,
A sharp nip in the morning air.
The hedgehog pokes his nose out,
The fox comes out of its lair.

Summer

Buckets and spades at the seaside,
The swallows are on the wing.
The kids are on their holiday,
On the roundabout and swing.

Autumn

The leaves are changing colour,
Some trees are looking bare.
The squirrels are gathering their nuts in,
They really are aware.

Winter

Jack Frost is making patterns,
He's really on the 'go',
The sky is looking grey now,
I guess it is going to snow.

Laura Bainbridge (12)
Emmanuel College

EMMANUEL COLLEGE

My first day here,
I got through it fine,
In fact I made new friends,
All of the time.

Our school Emmanuel,
What can I say?
Students' effort 100%,
Every hour of every day.

From year seven exams too
GCSE,
If we all revise hard,
We know we'll succeed.

When we're 18 years old,
We'll get a standing ovation,
Because we'll all come out,
With such high education.

Well this is our school,
Where we all do well,
This is our school,
Emmanuel!

Steven Fallon (12)
Emmanuel College

THE STAGES OF LIFE

School's a place where we have to go,
It's not a choice, we can't say 'No!'

At an early age of three or four,
You're being chased through the nursery door.

At the age of five when you start to learn,
Golden stars you begin to earn.

We start Junior School at the prime age of seven,
And we work really hard till the age of eleven.

At the age of eleven we start our new schools,
With this there's no problem apart from the rules.

At the age of eighteen, it's the hardest year yet,
Good exam results it's important to get.

As we go on our journey through the great unknown,
We sit back and think 'My, haven't we grown?'

Amanda Dawson (13)
Emmanuel College

FOOTBALL

Football is definitely my favourite game,
A lot of passion and a lot of pain.

Passing the ball and making a run,
When it goes right, it's a lot of fun.

Tackling players to win the ball,
Always shooting towards the goal.

Being fouled badly towards the ground,
Getting back up, it does astound.

The keeper dives to make a catch,
When the whistle blows it's the end of the match.

Paul Baptist (12)
Emmanuel College

MONDAY MORNING

I get up each morning,
just as the sun is dawning
and slowly fall out of bed.

'Morning!' shouts mother,
and then I discover, it's Monday
and jump back in bed.

'You'll be late, you'll be late.'
They'll shut the school gate,
And I know lessons won't wait.
But once in my bed,
I dream in my head,
Till mother comes shouting
'Get out of bed!'

Well I'm going in the gate,
and it's the bell that I hate,
'cause it's ringing to tell me,
'Wesley, you're late!'

Wesley Brunskill (12)
Emmanuel College

COLOURS

The sky is blue,
The trees are green,
Wherever you go they're sure to be seen.

The sun is yellow,
The clouds are white.
The moon at night is always bright.

The stars are silver,
The rain is grey,
It doesn't rain very often,
Hip! Hip! Hooray!

Stephen Atkinson (12)
Emmanuel College

MIDNIGHT WOOD

Deep in a dark wood,
Owls hoot as anxious animals scurry
round trees for food.
Snorting and snuffling
Badgers go down deep holes to their sets.
Wolves howl,
Leaves crunch,
The wind whistles round the tree tops.
Dawn breaks through the bushes and trees.
Animals awake from their sweet dreams.

Jessica Greenhaff (11)
Emmanuel College

ALAN SHEARER!

A lan Shearer is great and so am I
L ow fat calories but an odd mince pie!
A nd even though he's good for all his teams
N ewcastle's been the best, man!
   Well, so it seems.

S o never mind Paul Ince or rubbish Andy Cole,
H e's the best so bless his soul!
E verybody knows him, especially me!
A lan's my best player, as you can see!
R emain at the 'Toon' for all his life!
E very goal he scores it's simply just right.
R oaring crowds last all through the night!

Robert Riddell & Craig Spence (12)
Kenton School

MY POEM

N ewcastle United are the best,
E ven better than all the rest.
W aving scarves and flags in the air,
C hants of Toon Army,
A nd dreams of Europe and silverware.
S hearer, Tino and Albert
T ino scores
L eaving the opponents in despair
E veryone is Toon Army mad,

U ncles, aunties even Grandad,
T op of the Premier League, would be grand
D alglish and his team the best in the land.

Kris Abbott (13)
Kenton School

THE TALL MOUNTAIN

The mountain is very tall.
It takes you to the sky.
You go higher than the
birds.
The clouds look fluffy but
you can't touch them.
The mountain keeps on
going on and gets bigger
and bigger.
You don't even know if
you are at the top.
It's so big you could climb
forever.
But then it ended.

Craig Stephen Duggan (12)
Kenton School

DAY AND NIGHT

I gaze at the stars
In the sky at night
They shimmer and twinkle
And shine so bright.

Then dawn comes quick
The sun shines bright
I can see through the mist
It seems so bright.

The moon comes upon us.
The rain pours down.
We fetch our umbrellas
But out come the clouds.

The wind starts blowing
Away goes the rain
Out comes the moon
It's night-time again.

Lyndsey Walton (12)
Kenton School

SCARBOROUGH

Scarborough beach
Scarborough town
Scarborough bay
Every day I say
Can we go out
To have something to eat?
A restaurant for dinner
Fish and chips for tea
Ice-cream for supper
That will do for me
When the days go by
It is good
Till the last day
I am sad
But I can come back
And I am glad.

Kayleigh Chalmers (12)
Kenton School

SKY

Red sky at night, shepherds' delight . . .
Red sky at dawn, shepherds' warning . . .
That's what people say . . .
The weather can change with a
glance of light.

6 o'clock in the morning the sky is blue
7 o'clock in the morning and the sun
is shining through.
8 o'clock, I wonder what clothes to wear,
9 o'clock, I have my summer clothes,
but, my hat and scarf too . . .

The weather is so changeable I don't
know what to do . . .
I take my barometer to give myself a clue.
I have my umbrella, my wellies too . . .
The pointer is going hot, cold, wind
then fair.
I may as well be walking round
in my underwear.

I wonder why so many holiday places
are held indoors, maybe they're
having the same problem I'm having.

> With the weather in England
> You're better off indoors!

Carley Laskey (12)
Kenton School

NEWCASTLE UNITED

N ewcastle United matches are great
E ven against Manchester United
W e won 5-0 and
C antona is rubbish
A gainst the Black and White and
S hearer is the *best*
T ino is up front with him
L ee is the captain
E ven when Beardsley is there

U nited are still the best
N ot even Juventus could beat
I an Rush's new team
T homasson is good but the
E xceptional Rob Lee is just the best
D alglish is the manager, the best manager
                                  you can get.

Stephen Wilkinson (12)
Kenton School

MOUNTAINS

Mountains are large
Mountains are small
I wonder if someone could
climb them all.
One is above all the clouds
The other is smaller than all
the crowds.

Paul Spence (12)
Kenton School

SOME DAY, SOME NIGHT

Some day I may run away,
Some day I may but not today.

Some night I might split away
Into the moonlight
Some night I might but not tonight.

Some night, some day
I might, I may
But right now I think I'll stay.

Claire Watson (12)
Kenton School

SEAGULL

The seagull curves his wings,
The seagull slants his eyes,
He says to the fish,
'You're wise staying down there,
Come up here and you're in for a scare.'

The seagull slants his wings,
The seagull dives his head,
He says to the fish,
'You better stay down there,
Or I'll rip off your head.'

The seagull flaps his wings,
He glides through the air,
He swoops down to catch his meals,
He loves to fly high in the sky,
And stare over our heads.

Mark Blanshard (12)
Killingworth Middle School

WHY DO WE HAVE WARS?

War is anger,
War is fear,
War is something not to be messed with.
People are killed,
People are wounded,
People are separated from their family and friends.
People are made homeless,
People even starve.
Nobody could want this to happen,
So why are wars still being fought?
Can they enjoy watching people die?
I doubt it.
The countries should unite,
And make the world a safer place.
It takes two to tango,
And two armies to fight a war.

Edward Hunter (12)
Killingworth Middle School

CATS

My best friend is a cat.
He sleeps all day on his favourite mat.
He goes out at night.
To play and fight.
He's king of his territory and proudly stands.
To watch and protect his own lands.
He cleans himself and grooms his fur.
When I stroke him, he softly purrs.
His miaow can reach the highest note
And I just love his black and white coat.

Katie Little (12)
Killingworth Middle School

REJECTION

It's started again,
The familiar sounds of the arguments below,
I huddle up in the corner of my bed,
Wishing it would all end soon.
The voices begin to get louder,
And the words begin to get meaningful.
The tears trickle down my face,
Hoping, praying for it to stop,
But I know it will last for eternity.
It's silent, she's gone,
I sit wondering why,
The tears get stronger, she's left
She never said goodbye.
Why has she left me?
She knows I won't cope.
All I can do, is sit, wait and hope.

Hannah Pearson (12)
Killingworth Middle School

DOLPHINS

Dolphins are really cool,
Not to be locked up in a pool.
Dolphins swimming in the sea,
That's the way it should be.
Don't lock them up, *No! Please no!*
They're worth more than that
                    stupid cruel show.

Jenna Morrison (12)
Killingworth Middle School

WHO, WHAT, WHERE?

A child once asked
His mum some questions
About things that people don't know.

Why were people born?
Why did the Dodo die?
Why do we sleep?

Who created earth?
Who will find this out?
Who will stop all the wars?

What if the earth explodes?
What if China falls apart?
What made the sloth go slow?

Will Jesus come back?
Will we travel in space?
Will I live to be 100?

Where did the sun come from?
Where will I die?
Where do lost people go to?

Does space ever end?
Does anyone care?
Does time ever stop?

'My dear, when we are dead
And others live on
The answers will be revealed,' his mum said.

Alexandra Palmer (12)
Killingworth Middle School

THE ROBBER THAT NEVER WAS!

I was listening to some music in my room,
when I heard my mum bellow from below.
I ran to the door shouting 'What is it mum?'
And she ran upstairs with a huge shotgun!
'There's a robber trying to break in next-door'
I looked out my window and sure enough there was a man
the same height as our neighbour.
All dressed in black with a peculiar hat,
he slipped the credit card through the gap,
and pushed the door wide open.
He was in for five minutes or more,
and rushed out with a bag and closed the door.
'Oh who's that person going over?'
'Oh no, it's my mum with her shotgun.'
I ran downstairs shouting 'Wait a minute mum
that person looks rather familiar.'
Out pounced the cat and knocked off his hat,
And sure enough it was our neighbour!
What a lucky escape!

Laura McGill (13)
Killingworth Middle School

THE GAMES

Sprinters flying down the straight.
Hurdlers leaping over each jump.
The javelins cruising through the air.
Each spectator focusing, looking for an exclusive
But each and every contestant wants
       the same thing, the glory to win.

Flowers given out
Three colours of medals accepted.
Gold, silver and bronze.
Gold is the colour that everyone wants,
But only the winners can win.

Chris Bowe (12)
Killingworth Middle School

MY DAD'S DOG

My dad's dog
She's called Lady
But sometimes
She's marvellous
But then she's
Completely barmy.

When you enter
She goes nutty
But when you leave
She cries and cries
When you enter again
She's happy again.

My dad's dog
She's called Lady
But sometimes
She's marvellous
But then she's
Completely barmy.

Sarah Hindmarch (12)
Killingworth Middle School

BASKETBALL

We all come on to start the game
The other team looking lame
The game tips off, the ball goes high
The players jump up to the sky
We get the ball, we do something fast
The ball goes in their half at last
I take a shot, it hits the rim
I can't believe it, it's gone in
The exciting game starts again.
Oh it's tragic, they've done the same
Now the score is ten all
In this game of basketball
The players run to and fro
There's only five minutes left to go
We need another basket desperately
Who will score it, maybe me
I take a shot, it hits the rim
I can't believe it, it's gone in
The bell goes off, the game is won
But the bell keeps ringing on and on
My alarm clock's ringing that's a shame
That's the end of my *claim to fame!*

Ross Lindsay (12)
Killingworth Middle School

TRANSPORT

buses buses everywhere
their continuous service
goes everywhere
there are trams, trolleys
and school buses too
and even some with a
little loo

trains trains stick to one
route
there are steam trains
high-speed trains and
underground ones too
some go along the coast
the passengers use any
transport
or get the ferry and wait at the port.

Allen James Jamieson (12)
Killingworth Middle School

HAMSTER

I'm fast asleep,
Just lying there,
In the room above my house.
I wake up at the rattling,
Of the cat that's at the lock,
But luckily that girl is here,
To shoo that big mean cat away.
Up and up I'm lifted out,
Oh no! It's that mean boy,
Who aggravates and teases me,
And treats me like a toy.
Up and down and round and round,
I fall off and hit the ground,
But luckily that girl is here,
To pick me up,
Put me back in my cage.
I'm back in my room,
Sleeping once again.

Sarah Cuthbertson (12)
Killingworth Middle School

TIGER

Eyes like beams hunting for the prey,
don't bother running,
It will track you down,
night or day.
Teeth as sharp as a razor,
tongue licking its lips,
Searching for the flavour,
antelope, deer,
anything, to keep her cubs alive,
and from fear.
Its coat bold and bright,
Its orange hair so startling and outstanding,
It's enough to keep you awake at night.

Michael McNally (12)
Killingworth Middle School

DOGGIE DAYS

Doggie days are best by far
Snoozing on the kitchen floor
Eating doggie treats all day
Give us some more, that's the way
Take a walk in the park
See another dog and bark.
All day chasing next-door's cat
Go on, go on, go scat!
Here comes grumpy Mr Joe
Bite his bum, away you go
Lie down by the cosy fire
Luxury time, to your desire.
Now it's time to go to bed
Just lie down and rest your head.

Warren Gunn (12)
Killingworth Middle School

FOOD

I love food, I eat all day
I wouldn't have it any other way
Burgers and pies and pizza as well
I just love the way they smell
I eat food all the time
I start to eat at half-past-nine
In my mouth the food must go
As my stomach starts to grow
Cereal for breakfast, crisps for lunch
I just need to have a munch
When I come home my tea is great
It's all squashed on a giant plate
Cream buns and cakes they are so nice
I just have to have another slice
When I come home I look very dim
Because someone told me I need to slim
I'm very upset I'm starting to cry
As my river of food is beginning to dry
Very small dinners that's for me
But, as my stomach shrinks, my face fills with glee
I'm back to normal I can eat a lot
Yes, at this minute it's food that I've got
I've told you all this because I've nothing to hide
It's just I'm more happy with some food inside.

Andrew Sears (12)
Killingworth Middle School

BEING AT THE GRAVEYARD AT MIDNIGHT

The clock strikes midnight,
As the howls begin,
If you are going to the grave,
You had better be brave,
Because you could have a fright,
At this time of the night,
It suddenly begins to rain,
As ghosts start reappearing again,
Suddenly you will become cold,
As all the ghosts are old,
You turn to run,
Then there's the sun,
Night has gone,
Daylight has begun.

Nichola Baker (13)
Killingworth Middle School

GRANDAD

My Grandad is kind, gentle
he's so soft, and cuddly,
he sits smoking his pipe in his rocking chair.

My Grandad sits, and puts me on his lap,
and tells me his old war stories
as he rocks back and forth in his rocking chair.

My Grandad sits in his chair by the window
with a perfect view of the outside world
as he smokes his pipe and tells me
'One day son, you'll be as old as me.'

James Walker (12)
Killingworth Middle School

SNOWFLAKES

Snowflakes are falling,
heavy, light.
Falling swiftly all through the night.
What makes snowflakes travel so?
Will you or I ever know?

Snowflakes are landing,
on the ice.
Melting, melting, they don't think twice.
What happens to them now they're gone?
Will they come back one by one?

Snowflakes are landing,
on the snow.
Nice and gently the wind does blow.
Goodbye snowflakes! On you go!
We'll miss you more than you will know.

Katherine Palmer (12)
Killingworth Middle School

FEELINGS

Think and feel is what we do,
Run, skip and hop too.
Bigger, better than before,
Like a pebble on the shore.
Don't just sit and stare,
Life isn't always fair.
Please learn to care and love,
Don't just push and shove.
We'll care no matter what,
Go on, give it a shot!

Kelly Hardy (12)
Killingworth Middle School

DINNER LADIES

Dinner ladies on the go
Here they come, watch out!
Dinner ladies on the go,
How they scream and shout!

Robert chews cold cabbage,
Claire is eating chips,
Sue slurps up spaghetti,
Tracy's spitting pips.

Gill has left her lettuce,
Gav throws bits of pie,
Joan Bull peels an orange,
- Squirts juice in her eye.

Dinner ladies on the go
Here they come, watch out!
Dinner ladies on the go.
How they scream and shout.

Jim has turtle pizza
Courtney drains a Coke
Heather's sarnies make her
Splutter, cough and choke.

Andy drops his lunch box
- Food across the floor
Suddenly the cook shouts
'Seconds, who wants more?'

Dinner ladies on the go
Here they come, watch out!
Dinner ladies on the go
How they scream and shout!

Kaylee McCoy (12)
Killingworth Middle School

THE SECRET WEAPON

It's nearly time, boots on
The manager tells us one by one
The position we are going to play
It's the same as any other day
But today football will be a different game
As we unleash him and give him fame
Our secret weapon
The goal-scoring machine.
The team gets ready for the whistle to blow
The opposition don't know what they're in for
The whistle blows we play it up the wing
The excitement grows, the crowd starts to sing
Our attacking mid-fielder number four
Sees the chance for him to score
The winger sends in a swerving cross
'Go for it son,' shouts the boss.
Number four pulls his foot back
And drives it in with a smack.
The keeper didn't have a chance
To celebrate we did a dance
The whistle blows it's the end of the half
But our star striker has a badly-pulled calf.
Our secret weapon is about to come on
Their chances have now certainly gone.
He scores a second, third and then
A pass comes in from number ten.
He sees the keeper off his line
And tries a lob, it's doing fine.
The ball goes in, the match is won
Our secret weapon's work is done.

Barry Morton
Killingworth Middle School

FOOTBALL IS LIFE

Sunday morning is the time
I get up at quarter to nine
I get my boots my shin pads too
I'm off to the game I love to play,
Football, football, that's the way.
I cross the ball with my right foot
It lands upon our striker's nut.
Into the net it begins to fly
As the opposite team starts to cry.
The half-time whistle is about to blow
Off the pitch we must go.
Our manager shouts to cheer us on
As he tells us what to do one by one.
They kick off the second part
Our central mid-fielder must depart.
Our wicked sub must come on
Their chance of winning has surely gone.
We swing the ball round and round
But eventually it hits the ground.
Our super sub volleys it in
The opposition's chances are now very slim.
The final whistle is blown right now
As we take an honourable bow.
The match is won by two goals to nil
That's the way it's been and it always will.

Kevin Hodgson (12)
Killingworth Middle School

SEASONS

Spring is a pain
When there is rain.
Summer is great,
When you have a mate.
Autumn is bare,
As it blows all my hair.
Winter is cold,
There is snow that I hold.

Summer is best,
Better than the rest,
Summer is fun,
When we go for a run.
I switch on the fan,
For my suntan.
I go beetroot red,
Including my head.

The year will not be the same
                    without seasons,
As there are reasons.
The leaves that fall,
And the odd snowball,
The sun glazing day by day,
Spring, which happens in May.

Seasons!

Rebecca Bull (13)
Killingworth Middle School

Zoo

That zoo that zoo,
Let's all go to the zoo,
Llamas, camels, gorillas too,
Animals, snakes, birds and spiders.
Ferocious lions, king of the jungle
Locked up.
Animals' cages,
Doesn't seem fair,
Elephants in small enclosures
Us running free
Them locked up
Again not fair
In the jungle animals,
Running free,
Bars,
Another one in the zoo
What can we *do?*

Phillip Burns (12)
Killingworth Middle School

Chester - My Pet

He has ears like aeroplane wings,
a nose like a button,
eyes like two beads,
lips hang down as if he's fed up,
but his wagging tail shows he's not.
His teeth stick out,
and his tongue is like a diving board.
He's a boxer dog.

Stuart Abbott (12)
Killingworth Middle School

MY DAD'S DEATH

When I heard *the news,*
I started to cry,
I didn't have time to say goodbye,
I saw him one day,
He was gone the next,
I am glad to have known him,
He was the very best,
And always will be.

It came to the day,
When the funeral was due,
It was like I had terrible flu,
It felt like he was there,
Holding my hand,
Trying to make me understand,
That although I could not reach out and touch him,
I will always be in his heart,
And he will always be in mine.

Nikki Irving (12)
Killingworth Middle School

THE WINTER WE ALL WISH FOR

Christmas is like an excursion,
Curl up in bed like a hibernating badger,
Step into the white, crisp snow,
Go skating on the glistening sheet of ice,
Go sledging down the white-cloaked mountainside,
Wake up to a room full of presents.

Jessica Weightman (12)
Killingworth Middle School

WORLD WAR

In 1939 war was declared
Everyone around was so scared.
Hitler's army did attack,
Then the English fought them back.
Bombs landed here and there,
Then explosions everywhere.
Loud noises, shooting, screaming
All the women's eyes were streaming.

Spitfires flying high and low,
Looking for lights down below.
Sirens go off, one, two, three,
Blackouts start, please save me!
Lights come on, look around,
There is my mother on the ground.

Sitting in the bunkers, wet and cold,
Sitting there until I was told.
Then I have the biggest fright,
The war was over at eleven o'clock.
Wasn't that six years of shock?

Dawn Fuller (12)
Killingworth Middle School

WAR

Rattle, rattle,
Fizz, fizz,
They're the sounds you hear,
Men screaming, black smoke,
Babies crying, children choke,
As large tanks trundle through
Shrapnel flying, bodies too.

All is dark, no more sound,
Bloody corpses cover the ground.
Even though people pray the peace will
never keep.
And already too many people are
in eternal sleep.

Andrew Yeats (12)
Killingworth Middle School

WORK

In my kitchen early,
Cooking a lovely breakfast,
Doing all the housework,
Tidying up the bedrooms,
     Work, work, work
Making up the lunch,
Washing all the dishes,
Cleaning down the benches,
     Work, work, work,
Doing more cooking,
I don't like cooking,
Doing more washing,
I don't like washing,
     Work, work, work,
Going out to work,
Back into the kitchens,
Cooking more foods
Sweeping down more benches
     Work, work, work,
Eventually I shut the shop
Then go back home to bed
I go straight to sleep.

Ben Wolf (12)
Killingworth Middle School

DIVORCE

Divorce is bad,
It makes me really sad,
I cried like torrential rain,
Over and over again.
I protested and protested again,
But it was too late.
Divorce.
My brothers did react too,
They did not cry.
They argued over and over.
They were angry, so angry.
They shouted as loud as possible,
They slammed doors, broke
Furniture
But the worst of all was Mam,
She sat with her friends
Drinking wine.
She got cards and presents,
But we couldn't do anything
About it,
It was over forever!
No more playing in the
Garden,
No more going to feed the
Ducks,
No more Dad!

Jill Boardman (12)
Killingworth Middle School

WHO ARE FRIENDS?

A friend is a person,
A friend ain't a thing,
A friend isn't something,
You keep inside a tin.

A friend can be young,
A friend can be old,
A friend can be tall,
A friend can be small.

But a friend,
If a real friend,
Likes you,
For who you are!

Diane Douglass (13)
Killingworth Middle School

WE'RE FOOTBALL CRAZY

Football is good, or could be bad,
When the ref blows the whistle,
The players go mad,
Shearer celebrates,
The ref blows again,
The crowd go wild when Shearer gets booked,
He tries not to swear,
But couldn't keep it in,
The ref just says 'Right get yourself in,'
The players don't believe it,
So they abandon the game,
Nobody believes it so they never played again..

John Alexander (12)
Killingworth Middle School

THE CAR POEM

Cars are long, cars are small
One of the biggest cars of all
Is not so weeny, not so teeny,
It's a fiery red Lamborghini.

Cruising down the motorway
                    100 miles an hour
We met the rain in a heavy shower
Crashing, spinning like a top
We hit the oil and couldn't stop.

My lovely luscious Lamborghini
Is now the size of a tiny Mini
No longer, long, no longer red
I had to put my car to bed.

Adam Mills (12)
Killingworth Middle School

FANG THE VAMPIRE RABBIT

There is no living thing with such a habit,
As sucking the blood like the vampire rabbit,
He turns away from lettuce and carrot,
And makes a noise like a squawking parrot,
When his keepers go to give his feed,
He snaps at their fingers for his greed,
They dare not risk getting too near,
As this will make them tremble with fear,
This seems to trigger his thirst for blood,
If he could bite them he surely would,
This would of course absolve his appetite,
And keep him happy throughout the night.

Darren Smith (12)
Killingworth Middle School

THE BIG CATCH

Fishing is a waiting game.
Sometimes it gets rather tame.
If you sit there all night.
And the fish refuse to bite.
Then some top anglers say.
'It's just not your day.'
You try again, you sit and wait.
Your watch stops, you're home late.
'What can I do?'
I aint got a clue.
Try a new bait.
A heavier weight.
The list goes on and on.
'You know what mate
Just try again, some day you'll get a fish.'
The day arrives,
He rushes into the bar.
'Lads, 'ave got a 20 pound carp'
The boy is wild.
He doesn't sleep all night.
This fish has stirred him up.
He develops his photos, engraves a cup.
He will never give up.
Well fishing is a waiting game.
Rather boring, rather tame.
You won't catch a thing,
Well some say.
But just you wait for that day.
When your float goes down.
And you begin the struggle.
To bring in your fish.

Iain Kennedy (12)
Killingworth Middle School

FISHING-ROD

It was one fine sunny afternoon,
And I was standing in the yard.
I turned around and realised that
I had a fishing-rod.
I walked down to the lake and
cast my rod out quickly.
I caught a giant fat juicy drake!

Its feathers all velvety, colours
of white and grey.
Its legs were all scaly like a
slithery snake.
I took my duck home and placed it
in the yard,
I showed it to the cat, it froze really
hard.

The sun was blazing high up in the
sky.
As I walked to the door, I heard a
bang, then a cry.
I turned around and on the floor,
I saw the duck alive no more.
I saw the feathers, blood and all,
My poor little drake a bedraggled
ball.

The evil cat has done its deed,
it won't be back that's guaranteed,
I dug a hole ten foot deep,
I placed it in and now it can sleep
(in a deep unwakeable sleep.)

That darn cat I could have killed
it there and then.
And now it's gone and that's
the end.

Emma Bayliss (12)
Killingworth Middle School

THE VAMPIRE

There's that creaking noise again,
I think it's coming back again,
It came last night or so they say,
Now Tommy will never see the light
of day.

No garlic, no cross would frighten
him off,
Just a stake through the heart would
finish him off,
His razor-sharp teeth, like those of a shark,
Bite through the skin like a flash in the
dark.

He slips out into the night looking
for victims to give a deep bite,
He charms the women with his
Brilliant smile,
Makes them go weak with the glints in
his eye,
He entices young children with tales
of gore,
Then picks the right moment to give
them a claw.

Natalie Angelopoulos (12)
Killingworth Middle School

THE CAT

Slowly but steadily he creeps
through the long silky grass.

He circles a certain tree with
pink petals and dark green leaves.

His white fur gleams in the sun
he waggles his tail from side to
side as he waits.

He can detect anything then
it comes. *Swoosh! Swoosh!*

His claws hook the bird and
it falls with a thud.

He scoops it up with his
razor-sharp teeth and walks
with proud steady short steps.

Ian Black (12)
Killingworth Middle School

AUTUMN

Fresh dew carpets the morning,
red painted skies, mark day dawning.
An abundance of colour flutters with the breeze,
amber, red and gold is whisked from trees.
Red, ivy veins creep up house sides,
north wind is gushing, mad and wild.
Wrapping around us, long dark night,
winter is well within sight.

Samantha Turnbull (12)
Killingworth Middle School

SHEEP'S REVENGE

Sheep are so peaceful,
Eating grass all day,
They face lots of dangers,
Journeying on their way.

They get chased by dogs,
And killed by foxes,
And the shepherdess just kills them,
And sells them in boxes.

But there are some cows,
Who are friends with the sheep,
And they killed the shepherdess,
Known as Little Bo Peep.

Alan Prior (12)
Killingworth Middle School

WAR AND PEACE

Anger is red,
Anger is lightning,
Anger is war,
Anger is frightening.

Once anger is over,
Calm appears,
Forgive and forget,
Perhaps a few tears.

Now the worst's over,
Let friendship return,
Enjoying ourselves,
A lesson to learn.

Daniel Pace (12)
Killingworth Middle School

CAPTIVITY

The bird in the cage began to cry
Because up in the sky she would
never fly
And as she sat in her cage at
night
She pushed the door with all
her might
Then one fine day, the door
broke open
No longer would she sit there
moping
And as she flew high in
the sky
No longer would she need
to cry!

Tracy Lough (12)
Killingworth Middle School

THE FRUSTRATED TODDLER

I sit and think
My pen won't write
No matter how long I sit
No matter how long I think
The page stays blank
My pen seems to have run out of ink
I just cannot write
I give up and come back later
I still cannot write
I might as well be trying to write with the wrong end of my pen
I might as well face it, I cannot write
But I am only two.

Christopher Sexton (12)
Killingworth Middle School

MY SISTER

I have a little sister
I think she's crackers
She calls herself Ackas
Why she does, I just don't know
Her real name is Alex

She watches the Teletubbies,
Tinky Winky, Dipsy, Laa-Laa and Po,
Why she does, I just don't know.

She stands on my bed
She jumps on my head
She won't get dressed,
She really is a pest,
But I couldn't be without her,
She really is the best
Why I think this, I just don't know.

Daniel Jeffrey (12)
Killingworth Middle School

WHO DID IT?

Wouldn't it be lovely to be a tree
All the branches swaying
Company at hand
But wait a second
Where's the tree gone?
It couldn't have disappeared
Oh no, it's on the floor
It must have been torn
'But who?' I utter, 'Could have done that?'
'Me you nutter.'
A tree cutter!

Elizabeth Henzell (12)
Killingworth Middle School

MY LONELY LIFE

My alarm clock rings
I look around
There isn't a soul, not a sound
I make my bed from only one side
This loneliness I can't abide
I look outside to see the kids playing
I can only imagine, what they're saying
I go to school to listen and learn
But instead I get taunted in turn
The teachers think I am bright
But not as noticeable as the boy on the right
Then come the names the kids will call
Fatty, four-eyes, ginger and all
It's 3.30pm it's time to leave
Where do I run, who will believe?
I run to my mum,
'I haven't got time, I'm going to work, you will be fine'
I'm back to square one, all alone
No one to talk to, no one to phone
I can take no more,
My life has no meaning
I know I'm a bore
But I too have feelings.

Vaughan Morrow (12)
Killingworth Middle School

HALLOWE'EN

October 31st Hallowe'en is here,
A full moon shines in a dark, dark sky,
Shadows of witches on brooms appear,
Cats, which are black, perched on their
broom as they fly.

126

Children dressed up as ghosts,
Making noises, oh how frightening,
Haunted house with skeletons as hosts,
Devils breathing out fire like lightning.

Louise Mullen (12)
Killingworth Middle School

THE LONELY WIND

I make funny noises
I make things shake
I make trees sway
But no matter what I do, I'm ignored
I hear laugher
I hear everything but unseen
No matter where you look
No matter where you go
I'll be there
Sometimes I am strong
Sometimes I am weak
Sometimes I am cold
Sometimes I am warm
But I am lonely
No one to talk to
No one to comfort me
I might as well not exist
For I cannot enjoy anything
Like Christmas.

Adam Sexton (12)
Killingworth Middle School

THE ULTIMATE EXPERIENCE

Waiting with anticipation,
Will my turn ever arrive.
I hear the screams of excited children
As they begin the ride
It's my turn next.
A shiver runs down my spine.
Shall I, shan't I? That is the question.
Is it too late to change my mind?
'Go on be brave,' a voice inside says.
'Climb aboard, give it a try.'
It's too late now, it's time to get on.
'Brace yourself for the ride of your life.'

Rachel Emma Cleghorn (12)
Killingworth Middle School

AWKWARD QUESTIONS

My Ma thinks she
knows everything.
Why is it then, I want
to know
Whenever I ask this
question.
Her eyes pop out, her
mouth gapes wide,
Her face goes red, she
swells inside?
I'll try again, here I go,
'Ma . . . where do
babies come from?'

Zoe Chow (12)
Killingworth Middle School

THE HORRIFIC WITCH

In the middle of the night
There is a really horrific sight.
I discovered a green hairy witch
She is really quite a titch
Round and round the cauldron she goes
Stirring the pot on her tip-toes.
The witch is wearing a pointy hat
And has a rather dodgy black cat
She is wearing a silky long cloak
But she is with a handsome bloke.
Then softly she spoke:
'Hocus, pocus, turn around
From the top to the ground'
I knew a spell was about to be cast
So I ran for the exit, very fast.

Vikki Teruel (12)
Killingworth Middle School

SHADOWS

I walked along the street one night,
With only the moon and its gentle light.
I met someone who wasn't there,
Yet it followed me around everywhere.
Around the corner, up the lane,
Feeling the patter of the autumn rain.
I reach my drive and up I run,
It's still behind me, having fun.
It even invited itself into my home,
But when I looked back, it had gone.

Christine Wilson (12)
Killingworth Middle School

SEA

The sea is a clear, deep, blue sea,
In which I can see a reflection of me.
The reflection I see sparkles all day and night,
And reminds me of rainbows, all vivid and bright.

Sea urchins, crabs, prawns ever so small,
Compete with sharks, octopuses, fish ever so tall
The sea-bed full of animals and plants,
All merry and happy together they dance.

When I am in the sea, I play around,
While I listen to the splashing sounds.
Over the sea the ships do sail,
In all different weathers, sun, wind and hail.

Laura Pinfold (12)
Killingworth Middle School

CHEESE

Choosing cheeses always pleases
People with good taste.
Picking carefully a good Caerphilly
Would never go to waste.
When Wallace buys the Wensleydale
It makes young Gromitt wag his tail.
The Dutch build dikes, shouting louder
It will keep dry, their Edam and Gouda.
While further north, it may be true
That the cold weather makes the Danish blue
Camembert is soft and spready
Parmesan gets the pizzas ready.
Mozzarella, Ricotta a joy to see
But Feta is all Greek to me!

John Foggo (12)
Killingworth Middle School

MY HAMSTER'S WORLD

My name is Snowball
I have a cage with two floors
My food is all nuts
I am quenching my thirst with water
From a water bottle
I have a wheel to play on
I am going fast on it
'Great!'
Here comes my friend
He sticks his hand in my cage
Should I bite him or not?
His hand is coming nearer
Should I? Should I?
'Course I wouldn't
He picks me up and strokes me
He plays with me for a while
Before he goes to school
He feeds and waters me
I have a white fur bed
It is lovely and warm
It is hard to see me
I am a white teddy bear, hamster
You can see my black ears
My red albino eyes as well
Lovely bed, soft, warm and all mine.

Ashley Proctor (12)
Killingworth Middle School

THE PENALTY

The crowd was quiet,
If he scored there would be a riot.
There wasn't long to go,
Would he put it high or low?
If the keeper saved the ball,
It would remain one-all.
He started his run-up, he looked
very tense,
The referee blew his whistle
and broke the silence.
He took 4 paces, his foot struck
the ball,
Wham! He scored a goal.
A roar from the crowd,
Made the player, very proud.
All the keeper could do was pick up the ball,
In hope that his team mates
could make it two-all.

David Breeze (12)
Killingworth Middle School

THE POUND

All alone in the pound,
quiet, smelly, not a sound.
In the morning you will hear the sound,
of barking everywhere.
In my cage I lie and stare, watching,
people standing there.
Walking by and shouting loud,
kiddies running round and round.

They all walk by and look at me,
I wish they'd take me home for tea.
I lie there every day and night,
watching them turn out the light.
Instead of sitting like a gnome,
I've found myself a lovely home.

Sean Murphy (12)
Killingworth Middle School

CHAOS

You should see my house in the morning,
I get up and everyone's snoring,
When they all wake, they all start to panic,
Whatever they're doing, oh my goodness
they're late!
My grandad comes out from the attic,
And my mum stumbles out of the gate,
The dog gets the kitchen all dirty and wet,
Then my dad flies in to clean up the mess.
He hasn't washed, he hasn't shaved and he's
still in his jarmies.
There are bottles of wine on the table from
last night's party.
My sister stumbles over a mop and her breakfast
is all over her face,
It's pouring down with rain.
I'm out of the house, I set off for school
My house is in chaos again!

Sarah Bushbye (13)
Killingworth Middle School

FOOTBALL

Football, football it's a big game,
Football, football, no one will complain.
There's a big game, Newcastle V Bath,
You better watch, it will be a laugh.
There it starts, Bath in blue,
Have a look it's really true.
Newcastle come up like water,
Shooting out of a cup.
Cross, in by Shearer's lace,
Finished off by Asprilla's face.
We thought it was a phoney,
But it was really Pistone.
Robert Lee gives it a flick,
Then Shearer scores with a kick.
Newcastle score another goal,
Now Kenny knows we're in control.
David Batty gets a kick,
Now he feels really sick.
He goes off giving it a rub,
And here comes a new sub.
There Newcastle go with a
Huge big roar.
But for Bath, it's a terrible
Score.

Sean Beattie (12)
Killingworth Middle School

CHRISTMAS TIME

Christmas comes but once a year,
A happy time for most children
mostly everywhere.
Chocolates and sweets so many
lovely treats.
So many lovely treats.
The stuffing is piping hot,
and the baby's asleep in her cot.
Some parents are able to spend
hundred of pounds,
on gifts.
We fill to the brim,
and make ourselves fat.
Christmas comes but once a year,
a happy time for most children
mostly everywhere.

There are people we sometimes
don't see.
Homeless, the sick and dying,
please help them,
they're human too.
Give them food,
and treats if you can.
It's not for us,
celebrating without them.
Help them survive the hard
cold Christmas time.

Zara Regan (12)
Killingworth Middle School

HOUDINI THE HAMSTER

Dad's behind the wardrobe,
Mum's under the sink,
The hamster's on the loose again,
Things begin to stink.

We've looked behind the dresser,
We've looked under the stairs,
Things are getting tedious,
Like anybody cares.

It's starting to get dark now,
I want to go to bed,
The hamster's snug in a corner, asleep,
Wish it were me instead.

Hooray, we've found him, finally,
In amongst the dark,
And then the minute we get to bed,
We hear the dog's morning bark.

Elizabeth Jane Miller (12)
Killingworth Middle School

COLOURS

Yellow is for happiness,
Fresh and tasty.
Brown is for when the leaves
Fall in autumn time.
Blue is the ocean waves.
And white is for the Easter
Bunny in spring time.

Red is for anger,
Raging like fire.
Green is for the holly,
At Christmas time.
Orange sizzles like the sun.
Black is for mourning,
Reminds me of death.

Lyndsey Keene (12)
Killingworth Middle School

RESPONSIBILITIES

We are responsible for animals,
Not just cats and dogs,
But every animal,
Here and there.
Responsibilities!

Help animals,
Like Boots and Bodyshop,
They act responsible,
Just like we should.

Mad cow disease, BSE,
Whose responsibility? Naturally ours,
Use it, use it,
Just think.
Responsibility!

Samantha Jayne Wilson (12)
Killingworth Middle School

NEIGHBOURS AREN'T WHAT THEY USED TO BE

The bloke next-door is on your tail
In his Mazda MX5.
You run down the cut,
hop over a fence
and just manage to stay alive.
But here comes his wife,
she has cut you off
with the turbo-charged scooter from *hell!*
He drives through a hedge,
and knocks down a wall.
so under a fence you start to crawl.
So here you are,
wedged under a fence
with the psychos ready to pounce.
And all you did was pop next-door,
to ask for a sugary ounce.

Tom Lowenstein (12)
Killingworth Middle School

AUTUMN DAYS

Dark days are now approaching,
Cold frost lies upon the ground.
Leaves that crunch beneath my feet,
Lie all around, they clutter streets.
Trees that sway to and fro,
A swooshing, swishing they seem to go.
Lampposts light up autumn nights,
As birds take their last flights.
People hibernate in their homes,
As we all wait for winter storms.

Sarah Bennison (12)
Killingworth Middle School

NIGHT-TIME

I'm lying in my bed,
With my eyes still open.
I can't get to sleep,
I try counting sheep.
But all I hear is,
The taps dripping,
Dogs howling,
And my bathroom door creaking,
And cats crying.
Suddenly,
The clock strikes midnight,
Everything's silent,
I close my eyes.
Eventually I'm asleep.

Dawn Moulden (12)
Killingworth Middle School

YAPPING YORKIE

My little Yorkie, Dillon,
is a nasty little yapper!
He sits outside nearly all day,
guarding the garden,
come rain or shine.
He's black, brown and grey,
with a nose like a little button.
When he gets running,
his legs start thudding,
and if he sees a *cat,*
you *don't* want to hear him barking!

Louise Hutcheson (12)
Killingworth Middle School

ALL ABOUT ME

My parents find it funny.
When I fiddle about.
With little amounts of money.
My sister finds it amusing.
When I play a game.
And I'm losing.
My friends think it's cool,
When I'm playing well at pool.

But I think it's funny.
When my parents call me
'Honey.'
And when my sister's a nag.
I always think, what a drag.
And when I'm with my mates.
We never talk about interest rates.

And if I had no mam and dad.
I would be.
An uncontrollable lad.
And if I had no mate.
I wouldn't be able
To stay out late.
So I thank you for.
Everyone I know.

Dean Collins (13)
Killingworth Middle School

I Am Crying

I am crying, almost dying
She was the best Princess of them all
The giant, the big, the medium, the small
Plus all the sick and poor she helped
While most others kept their money to themselves.
My heart was breaking
So painfully aching
All the evening I sat there and cried
For I knew Princess Diana had died.
She had quite a good life, that is all I can say
But one day she sadly passed away
So, Heavenly Father up above, take care
Of her and give her your love.
So we'll all remember that sad day
When the world's best Princess passed away.
We'll always love her and always care,
For in our hearts she's always there.

Julie Hunter (13)
King George Comprehensive School

In My Room

I'm sitting in my bedroom staring at the wall
The computer's gone barmy, telly and all.
Listening to music, it's Elton John.
Singing the record for Diana who's gone.
Diana's our Princess, our English rose.
But she'll be queen in Heaven or wherever she goes.
She's loving and tender, a person who cares.
She'll miss William and Harry, but we'll say our prayers.

Rachael Watkins (13)
King George Comprehensive School

WATCHING THE CLOCK

Sitting in the classroom
staring at the clock,
listening to the sound of it
going tick tock tick tock.

Finally the bell rang
everyone rushed out,
running down the corridor
straight into the science lab.

Sitting in last lesson
doing experiments,
lighting Bunsen burners
thinking what to do.

Finally it was home time
and everyone felt great,
because after all that hard day's work
the bell had finally rung.

Rachel Hilburn (11)
King George Comprehensive School

UNTITLED

I was in my bedroom one night
I looked outside
There was no one there
There were no cars, no trucks
Nothing in sight.

It was cold
It was windy
It was snowy
I couldn't see anything, no one in sight
Just a snowman alone in my garden below

Natalie Walker (12)
King George Comprehensive School

THE CHANGING TREE

It's springtime now,
The frosty mornings have begun,
The shoots sprout from the ground,
And the tree begins to grow.

It's summertime now,
The sun is smiling,
The leaves begin to spread,
And the bird's nest is in the branches.

It's autumntime now,
The weather is changing,
As the leaves change colour,
They tumble to the ground.

It's wintertime now,
The snowflakes flutter,
The snow lies on the bare branches,
As the wind blows wildly.

Laura Pescod (11)
King George Comprehensive School

MY WORLD

My name is Daniel Bertram
I live at Caraway Walk
My sister is a pain in the neck
So I would like to hit her with a fork

The garden is like a jungle

In which monkeys would like to play
When my mum cuts the lawn
It takes her all day

The Estate is fast and furious
There are lots of people to see
It's almost like a race track
And when I walk out the door
People zoom past me

My favourite hobby is skating
I love it so much
It's like I am the cheetah chasing its prey
That is why I like it a lot

My family is like the ocean
It's spread across the world
They come from far and wide
So I have been told.

Daniel Bertram (11)
King George Comprehensive School

FOOTBALL IS MY GAME

Football is my favourite sport,
I love it, yes I do.
If I put on the England strip,
It will be my dream come true.

I'd love to be a pro one day,
'Cos winning is my aim.
I'd like to score loads of goals,
'Cos football is my game.

Adam Smith (11)
King George Comprehensive School

THE DREAM

Lying on the bed of dreams,
drifting to a place where nothing is what it seems.
Where I am swimming in a long, deep lake.
Refreshing, cool, I never want to wake

Where mysterious things, they happen to me.
Little magic men with four legs, I see.
Men with humps on their backs,
with pain and suffering, lift up their sacks.
Fairies flying in circles, bright colours they make,
fly to a castle to see the princess awake.

I'm in a place where people never go to bed,
Where ladies dance around, holding their head.
Where babies, dance, play and walk,
they sing, tumble, squeal and squawk.
A place where I am what I want to be.
A place where I see what I want to see.

Where the men bear children and the
women are all strong.
I think I am bad, a monster, am I wrong?
Suddenly I'm scared, confused, I shake.
I open my eyes, now I'm awake.

Kelly Warren (13)
King George Comprehensive School

IN MY DREAMS

When it's dark and no longer light,
I wonder what I'll dream tonight,
I could be a bird and glide in the sky
and sit on Big Ben way up high
I could be a flower and smell so nice
or be eaten slice by slice,
But I won't think about that now
For I could even be a cow,
What a silly thought,
I could be a spaceman and fly to different planets
or I could be eaten by a thousand gnats
So I hurry to my spaceship and fly back to Earth
I could even live in Hollywood and bowl or shop or surf,
I could have anything I wanted, even a mansion of my own,
Inside I would have money, gold and precious stone,
So I get back into bed and crawl under my sheet
And quickly close my eyes and hurry back to sleep.

Kimberley Knowles (13)
King George Comprehensive School

UNTITLED

It was the first day of school
It was cold and there was snow on the ground
As the children ran through the playground
My heart filled with joy.
I forgot about my mum and ran to join them
Not long after the bell went
And everything went quiet
The yard was empty
And I began to cry,

Donna Raine (14)
King George Comprehensive School

IMPORTANT TO ME

Chips and ketchup
Biscuits and tea
These are some things that are
important to me
Playing my CDs very loud
singing along
Playing football all day long
Taking my time whilst having a bath
Playing with my sister and making her laugh
But they are things that are important and fun
But what about the serious
things like - is my homework done?

Adam Anderson (11)
King George Comprehensive School

UNTITLED

A face of an angel,
She was a breath of fresh air,
She held such a beauty inside and out,
You couldn't help but stare.
A Queen of people's hearts
As she was known by.
A loss by the nation
As millions cry.
Goodnight sweet Diana,
Forget you we will not,
Because out of all the Royals
You were the best of the lot.

Jill Bradbury (13)
King George Comprehensive School

QUEEN OF HEARTS

She was a young shy girl
Who fell in love like a pearl,
A fairy tale wedding,
With two young sons,

But all did not go according to plan,
Divorce was the answer to our dismay,
They finally went their own way.

She was our inspiration and cared for us all,
But now she is gone,
And we can't do much at all,
We'll treasure her memory for ever and ever
Until we float away like a feather.

She was a sparkling star, very bright,
They stay up all night,
We'll always remember her like a queen.

Now she rests in peace.

Sara Dehnad (14)
King George Comprehensive School

FOOTBALL

My favourite sport is football
I play it all the time
I watch it on the telly when
Ravanelli shows his belly.
Newcastle United, my favourite team
in the premier league.
With Alan Shearer on the team he
is always a mean machine.

John Nicholson (13)
King George Comprehensive School

THE PEOPLE'S PRINCESS

Diana, Princess of the people, she is in our heads day and night,
She stole our hearts, she was so bright,
Oh, Diana, the Queen of the night.
When people are sad or shed a tear,
Diana, the Queen of the heart, was always near.
She was loving, caring, peaceful and warm,
People loved her, Queen of us all.
Now she has gone, I shed a tear,
But I feel she is always near.

Donna Aynsley (14)
King George Comprehensive School

ME AND MY DOG

I have a dog called Max
his ears are full of wax
and I think everybody knows
he bites my toes because if
you stand at the gate
you can hear him barking.
Last year I had a pair of trainers
with a floppy tongue
He ripped the tongue off one of my trainers
and then I threw them away
and bought a new pair straight away.

Christopher Stobbs (12)
King George Comprehensive School

SPELLBOUND

Fire and flame
Smoke and heat
One warrior brave and strong
The flame cannot be quenched
For the human spirit is great

Water and ripple
Rainbow and colour
A princess gentle and kind
She cannot be broken
For the human soul has power

Both are mortal enemies
Yet both are spiritually one
They cannot be united
But they are bound
By the spell of love.

Kam Li Cheng (13)
King George Comprehensive School

THE WORLD

The world was an empty place
until people came on the land
There were boys, girls and animals too.

The world is not boring
There are colours everywhere
Like the grass that is green
and the yellow sun.

The world is a big place
with lots of countries
like Africa, Canada and more

The world is beautiful
There's more to see
So enjoy your life and have some fun.

Tracy Purvis (11)
King George Comprehensive School

SPELLBOUND

The rainbow colours draw your eyes,
You cannot move, quite mesmerised,
Your eyes move from end to end,
As you slowly follow the rainbow's bend.

Red, orange, yellow and green,
These are some of the colours I've seen.
Indigo, violet, beautiful blue,
Such depth of colours, such wonderful hues.

On the horizon, lie pots of gold,
Waiting for mystical powers to unfold.
Before we can move, before we can stand,
Billowing clouds then cover the land.

We watch as the wind hurries them on,
We turn to our rainbow, to find it has gone.
The colours, the hues, the gold are no more,
Our spellbinding visions were greatly flawed.

Overcome by a spell, a fascinating way,
My eyes open wide as my mind went astray.
The inspiration is gone the moment is lost,
Dumbfounded, amazed all at no cost.

Shelley Holliday (14)
King George Comprehensive School

DIANA

Diana, Diana
You are the Queen of Hearts.
When people were in need you were a friend indeed
You never hated, you only loved.
Diana, Diana, now in Heaven above,
People will always have love inside them
just as you loved us.
Diana, Diana, so good and so kind
We will always remember the day you passed away.
We hope you are still as precious in Heaven as
you were on earth.

Lee Bailey (13)
King George Comprehensive School

MY DOG

I have a dog who is big and black
But he is not fat.
Who would care if I didn't,
would my poor dog end up forgotten.
When he lies down
he looks like a bit of a clown
When he starts to mess about
I normally have to give him a clout.
He is a bit of a hog.
But that's all about my dog.

Alison Doyle (13)
King George Comprehensive School

THESE THINGS ARE SPECIAL

The thing which is special to me
Is the house in which I live.
People who are special to me are my
Brother, my mother and a dog named Bandit.
My bear is special to me
Because my dad gave it to me when I was three.

My friends are special to me
Because without them I would be lost and alone.
My old school was special to me
Because of the memories I have of it -
The friends and the teachers I left behind.

Daniel Child (11)
King George Comprehensive School

MY FAT BROTHER

A big lump of blubber
Has set upon my brother
I don't know why this blubber
Has set upon my brother
I love my little brother
He's my hunky hubba-bubba
He's a silly kind of brother
And it's hard to resist
A little poke at the blubber
In the middle of my brother.

Danielle Green (11)
King George Comprehensive School

MY FAMILY

I love my family lots and lots,
They mean so much to me,
I couldn't do without them,
I'd be like a flower without a stem.

My Dad goes to work every day,
So we can have a holiday,
He likes his garden in his spare time,
Especially when the sun shines.

My Mam works hard and very long,
Never doing anything wrong,
Then she comes home and does the cleaning,
She even reaches up and does the ceiling.

I have a brother, his name is Paul,
He drives me up and up the wall,
But still I love my family lots and lots,
Without them I would be lost.

Faye Mort (11)
King George Comprehensive School

SPELLBOUND

Magically floating in a world that doesn't belong.
Entranced inside a wicked spell, alone and no one to tell.
Dreaming, wishing, someone was so near, so that they could help,
to magically wish me away from here.
Magically floating in a world that doesn't belong.
I'm held inside this wicked spell forever, no one, ever, to tell . . .

Vikki Davison (13)
King George Comprehensive School

AUTUMN DAYS

When it is the autumn the leaves are lovely colours.
They are orange, brown, rust, red and yellow.
When you walk, they crunch under your feet,
while walking down the country lanes.

As the leaves fall in the gentle breeze, berries start to appear.
The colours of them are red on the rowan trees
and orange on rose hips.

The nights grow shorter and when people have been out
they are always glad to be in front of their warm cosy fire.

Laura Thorpe (11)
King George Comprehensive School

SPELLBOUND

Bewitched and floating
What is this place?
A dreamland that only exists
in my mind
At first trapped and cold
lonely, wanting to be set free.
Then mystery and fantasy
as peace floated through me
colours as a rainbow drifting
through clouds in this magic land.
A world I could live in forever.

Kirsty Parker (13)
King George Comprehensive School

SPELLBOUND

Fixated at the attractive features,
A winding ribbon of water,
Flowing like a flounce on a garment all ripples.
It proceeds smoothly though a large bouquet of greenery,
Almost in slow motion but yet time flies so quickly.
Entranced by the scenery surrounding me,
Situated on an incline,
Marvelled at what stands before me.
A narrow beam of light catches the stream,
Now like tinsel on a tree,
Caught in a spine shivering draught flowing with the
occasional twinkle.
Faced with clusters of tree of many kinds.
Such as oaks, acorn and conker.
Grass blowing in the wind,
Like animal fur blowing in the breeze, soft, silky and clean.
I sit very nearly hypnotised.
Entranced, delighted,
Spellbound.

Jennifer Ramsey (13)
King George Comprehensive School

SPELLBOUND

Riding along down the street,
Enchanted by people I meet,
Fantasising about what's ahead,
Mesmerised by words that are said.

Faster and faster along I go,
Mysterious faces I see high and low,
All my dreams come to an end.
When I fall off my bike going round a bend.

Beverley Balback (14)
King George Comprehensive School

SPELLBOUND

The music is so powerful,
The enchantment makes me dance,
As I move about so freely,
I feel I'm in a trance.

I feel I've found my freedom,
Locked in the notes they play,
Will the force let me go,
Within the present day.

The path is at my fingertips,
But yet so far away,
The music will not let me stop,
It wants me forever to stay.

I cannot fulfil this dream I had,
To listen to it 'till the end,
The spell has come to work on me,
But will it ever stop.

Nicola King (13)
King George Comprehensive School

FOOTBALL IN THE PARK

I play football in the park with all my mates.
Neil, Chris, Bob, Andy, Nathan and Mark,
It's my ball, so I'm in charge.
Andy and Neil both collide,
And to the ground they fall,
'Play on' I shout, 'Shoulder barge!'
And he got the ball!

I play football in the park every day,
I'm one captain, and the other is Mark,
My team always wins,
Again, and again, and again!

Jumpers as goal posts,
An imaginary box,
A dent for the penalty spot,
And I try with all the skill I've got.

My best mate is Neil,
And his speed is incredibly unreal,
He runs like a train,
His feet do the talking,
But the plan is in his brain.

Then there is Bob,
Who plays like a slob,
He's on theirs.
He's got a bad shot,
Which goes over the bar,
He has to go get it,
And it's gone dead far.

Chris is on ours,
And Nathan's in goal,
They have got Andy,
And his brother Mick,
And sometimes even their cousin Dick.

We win by a mile
An unrealistic score,
We don't think of the future,
Where we won't play anymore.

Malcolm White (13)
George Stephenson High School

FIRST DAY AT THE COMPREHENSIVE

First day at school, frantic,
Huge people, small people, people everywhere,
Classes, classes and more classes, too many for me,
Teachers, teachers, how many more could you fit,
Children, rushing and pushing why are they in such a
rush,
Where do I go now, oh please somebody help me,
Oh there's a teacher, wait, oh please help me,
Dinner time, dinner time the part I've been dreading,
Will the food be good, delicious or sick,
What am I going to choose, fast food or traditional, ooh
a menu!
The dining room's full, full to the brim,
School's nearly over, hip, hip, hooray!
Two lessons to go and a few minutes of break
Whistle has gone, French is next,
Un, Deux, Trois,
Only one more lesson to go
That lesson's over, hip, hip hurrah
The bell has gone!
Home time.

Jenny Cummings (11)
Ryton Comprehensive School

WITHOUT A HOME

Without a home
Out on the street
I move around
No place to sleep.

Without a home
Nowhere to rest my head
But a cardboard box
I use as a bed.

Without a home
No food to eat
No cap on my head
No shoes on my feet.

Without a home
Outcast, outside
And though people stare
I still have my pride.

Without a home
No family or friends
I live alone
In a world that never ends.

Without a home
Through rain or shine.
Yet, in a way,
The whole city is mine.

Anne Hardisty (13)
Ryton Comprehensive School

WITHOUT A HOME

Many years ago,
When I was only ten,
I ran away from the home,
Which I never saw again.

I was feeling pretty low,
So I wandered the streets,
Then I looked around and saw,
People dying at my feet.

I found an empty spot,
And unpacked my bag,
Had I done the right thing,
Or was I completely mad?

I thought of my mum,
And my father, poor man,
'Stay with us!' They desperately cried,
Before I turned and ran.

I see a happy girl,
Wishing it was me,
I bet she doesn't worry,
About her next cup of tea.

I pull my blanket closer,
I'm feeling so alone,
This is what it's really like,
When you're without a home.

Victoria Scott (13)
Ryton Comprehensive School

A HOMELESS LIFE

I lay on the pavement,
All alone,
It's full of sadness,
In the homeless zone.

People stroll past,
With money to spare,
I shout 'Ten pence,'
They give me a stare.

I feel so frightened,
I feel so cold,
You should see my jumper,
It's covered in mould.

I wish I had money,
To at least buy warm rugs,
But instead,
I turn to drugs.

I go to a shop,
And steal a drink,
I drown my sorrows,
Then have a think.

I fell over,
And split my head,
But at least tonight,
I will have a bed.

I wish I could get out,
Of this zone,
I wish, I wish,
I had a home.

Lauren Sweet (13)
Ryton Comprehensive School

WITHOUT A HOME

I wander lonely along the streets,
Without a home to go,
I scrounge around the bins galore,
To find a single bite.

People always stop and stare,
To see my tiny home,
For on a doorstep is my home,
With nothing else at all.

On cold, dark nights galore,
I nearly freeze to death,
For over me I have nothing but,
My holed, old winter's coat.

Without a home,
I start to think where will my life go,
I have no friends, no food, no style,
So where will my life go?

Lisa Highmoor (12)
Ryton Comprehensive School

WITHOUT A HOME

I live on the streets and in a cardboard box,
In Newcastle city centre, near the quayside docks,
Someone walks past and I ask for money,
She checks for change and gives me 5p,
I go to the hostels for something to eat,
But they are always closed and run down at neet.

The river Tyne is a nice place to excrete,
But midges bite your bum and your feet,
Never knowing where your next food will come from,
I guess I'm just waiting to explode like a bomb,
I watch people walk past me in the street,
Jealousy gets to me, in the moment of heat.

So now you know what life is like,
Now before I get angry, take a hike,
I'm not very proud of what I am,
And even in the street, I'm classed as a sham,
I can't claim benefit because I haven't a home
So only if, but no I'm without a home.

Chris Symonds
Ryton Comprehensive School

WITHOUT A HOME

People walked past her
They didn't care.
But I stopped to look,
Knowing I shouldn't stare.
She sat there with a vacant
Look upon her face,
Probably wondering where is
Her place.

I thought,
Where is her place in this big
Cruel city
On a doorstep
Should people take pity?

Yes this city should take pity,
She's covered with snow
With nowhere to go
But another doorstep
That's cold and wet
And perhaps a stray cat
To give her a little comfort.

I wonder if she steals
So she can eat meals
Should I give her money
Or maybe a jar of honey.

She's lonely and scared
Of whom she shares
The dark, gloomy street.
She only wants one thing
Someone to sing
Come stay here for the night
And everything will be alright.

Suzanne Jones (13)
Ryton Comprehensive School

WITHOUT A HOME

It was a cold dark night
The wind howled like a wolf-hound's bite,
And there he was, this rag-and-bone man
Sleeping in his cart, as quiet as a lamb.

As I approached he jolted up
Gave me a look and a grunt like a pup,
We stared and stared with not a blink
And as I began to move, he gave me a wink.

His face was all scraggy and his clothes were all torn
The look on his face, wished he'd never been born,
Then in his cart among all the junk
He looked around and pulled out a small wooden trunk.

We sat there and rummaged through all of his stuff
The photos, the memories he'd just had enough,
He looked at the moon and ushered me to go
I slipped away, I'm the only one to know.

Simon Roberts (13)
Ryton Comprehensive School

MY LONELY LIFE ON THE STREET

I keep asking myself *'Why me?'*
Why should I have to sleep on the streets.
It's cold, damp and nobody cares,
Passers-by don't seem to have money to spare.

I try to drown my sorrows with alcohol,
I know it isn't good for me.
Though it does seem to keep me warm at night,
My hopes of finding happiness are out of sight.

Sometimes I have to turn to crime,
Just to get some money,
It's wrong, I know but I need to eat,
Even if it's only some scraps of meat.

On the streets it's so lonely,
If only I had a friend.
I wish I had someone who loved me,
But there's no one that I can see.

How long can I go on living like this?
Time seems to go so slow.
In a cardboard box I sleep,
The only thing I have to keep.

I watch the people pass by,
They usually just ignore me.
Either that, or they just stare,
I know they really don't care.

Kathryn Bush (14)
Ryton Comprehensive School

IT'S A LONG, COLD NIGHT

It's a long, cold night in the city,
With onlookers who just stare at you with pity,
But they never seem to think,
That you've had no food or drink,
For it's a long, cold night in the city.

It's a long, cold night in the town,
And the others show unhappiness with a frown,
Have to turn to alcohol,
To drown my worries and my soul,
For it's a long, cold night in the town.

It's a long, cold night on the street,
Hoping that some people will give a treat,
Like some money or just a coin,
That could turn my life around,
For it's a long, cold night on the street.

It's a long, cold night in the doorway,
And other people just try to ignore you,
They know you feel the same,
There's no need to hide in shame,
For it's a long, cold night in the doorway.

But it's a long, warm night in a house,
With such silence that you may just hear a mouse,
With the fire burning on,
With such warmth that is so strong,
For it's a long, warm night in a house.

Amy Hocking (13)
Ryton Comprehensive School

WITHOUT A HOME

Sitting here alone,
With nowhere to go,
Watching people pass,
While I'm feeling very low.

During the winter months,
I sit and shiver,
Watching people pass,
My lips begin to quiver.

Feeling very hungry,
Without any food,
Just a few pennies,
Would make me feel good.

The night is drawing in,
I need to find a home,
But where shall I go,
Home, where is home?

Amy Leck (13)
Ryton Comprehensive School

WITHOUT A HOME

As I make my way through the blustery night,
My body struggling to stay warm,
I make my way towards the light,
My heart is suddenly torn.

The coldness enters my cardboard box but my body
is already frozen,
The will to live is suddenly gone,
As my body is engulfed in poison.

I feel peaceful now at long last,
I finally have a place that I can call my own,
So I can rest and forget my past,
Looking after those like me whose homes are
on garden lawns.

Rebecca White (13)
Ryton Comprehensive School

WITHOUT A HOME

You'll never really know,
How it feels to be so low,
Homeless, hungry, down and out,
Scared of every thump and shout.

Cold, tired, frightened to move,
But you don't know why, there's nothing to lose,
Your only friend, a dog, named Spot,
The only living thing, who loves you a lot.

You find an open hostel and shout hooray!
And hope there's a spare bed for today,
You enter the building feeling suddenly warm,
How you wish that this place was your real home.

They've found you a bed, but only for tonight,
You know you'll be leaving with the new morning light,
You fill up with food, and enjoy the good meal,
You can't explain how good it makes you feel.

It's morning now, and it's time to go,
You pack your few things, sadly, with woe,
All because you have nowhere to live,
You hope another hostel has a bed to give.

Leanne Ovenden (13)
Ryton Comprehensive School

WITHOUT A HOME

Sitting in my cardboard box,
Silent as a fox,
The cold sweeps through my body,
I have nobody.

I drink to drown my sorrows,
What could happen tomorrow,
Just for some food, some drink, some shelter,
Life's just a helter-skelter.

Turn to crime,
Right on time,
Get put in a cell,
Away from the outside hell.

David Murray (14)
Ryton Comprehensive School

WITHOUT A HOME

Sitting here watching people go by,
they just look at me and I want to cry.
They turn their head and look away,
but I just wish that they would stay.

I sit here and wait all alone,
how I wish that I was at home.
I want to run, I want to hide,
No one knows my pain inside.

People look at me in despair,
I want them to talk, I want them to care.
My hair's in tangles and my life's in a mess,
Oh, how I wish that I had an address.

Joanne Bradshaw (14)
Ryton Comprehensive School

WITHOUT A HOME

The city is a large place,
With bright lights and a lot of space,
Roads are busy, packed with cars,
But still I sit there under the stars.
Passers-by stare and gaze,
Passers-by kick up haze,
No food or love or money to share,
Just me and the world, pockets bare.

Out on the streets, life is hard,
No food to eat, my pride is scarred,
No shelter, no home, no money to spend,
Begging and busking for money to lend.
If only there was a permanent home,
Where I could stay, not having to roam,
For me to live with all others,
Who share the problem of no mothers.

If there was a home like this,
I would live and never miss,
My old life on the street,
A life of crime, no shoes on my feet.
My clothes are old and tell the tale,
Of life sleeping rough, with no trail,
To get through it, you have to be tough,
A life on the street is very rough.

Robert Hooks (14)
Ryton Comprehensive School

WITHOUT A HOME

My emerald ring glitters in the lamp light,
her fingers are battered and bare.
My nails are long and painted rosy-pink,
hers are dirty and bitten down.
My expensive dress is fashionable and pretty,
her rags aren't in fashion or very warm.
As I think of my duck-down pillows and duvet,
and then of her doorstep or cardboard box.
I live in a warm, safe house and never go without food,
but I can only imagine how she must feel without a home

I've eaten too much.
She eats too little, could die any day if she can't find food.
I wonder if she ever had a home or anyone who cares,
I have so many friends and family.
But she has no one,
no love and caring to lift her when she's down.
So I slip a ten pound note into her icy cold hand,
and walk away, saddened at what I've seen and felt.

Madeleine Gray (13)
Ryton Comprehensive School

WITHOUT A HOME

People come, but pass me by,
without a glance or even sigh.
If they look, it's as if I'm dirt
but they don't know inside I hurt.
I do have feelings and need a hug,
but I am treated like a mug.

I wander in the freezing cold,
nowhere to go, no one to hold.
I'd really like someone to care,
to rid this feeling of despair.
But no one wants to know me now,
all because of one stupid row

My will has gone, why should I survive,
no one cares if I stay alive.

Philippa Edge (14)
Ryton Comprehensive School

WITHOUT A HOME

I had a drinking problem and I lost my home.
I am so weak, I am all skin and bone.
I try all the hostels and they turn me down.
If I can't find a box, I'll sleep on the ground.

I hang around the streets with Bill and Buffy.
They busk in the tunnel and they're really scruffy.
In the streets, the hours feel like days.
I've got a few pets and they are strays.

People in the streets laugh and stare.
They sometimes give us money but they really don't care.
It's cold in the winter and hot in the summer.
Being without a home really is a bummer.

David Thompson (14)
Ryton Comprehensive School

WITHOUT A HOME

I'm what they call a 'beggar on the street',
I'm cold and dirty and smell really bad,
I have no home and no relatives,
I have been like this since a small lad.

In wintertime, I am scared and lonely,
I have friends who become ill and die,
I often worry I'll get so cold, I'll pass on,
All I've eaten today, was a cold pork pie.

It's summertime now and it's really heating up
I've made a new friend who'll keep me from being lonely,
The weather is hot, it's like living on Venus,
It's times like this, I wish I had parents, if only.

Times are tough, so I turn to crime,
I've made a small amount of menacing money,
Now a drugs man gives me a chance to get hooked,
I try a little; not hooked, just feeling funny.

Now I'm really feeling the pain of being homeless,
Jealousy is seething through my body, at the rich, not the poor.
Yes, I live in a cramped, crummy cardboard box,
People laugh and stare at me, my life sucks, for sure.

Martin Wadham (14)
Ryton Comprehensive School

ANOTHER NIGHT

I walk on the hard street.
Without shoes on my feet.
I sleep in a bush at night.
Without a care about life.

My hair is old, battered and grey.
My clothes are rags.
My face is wasting away.

If I could have money again.
To rid me of my sorrow and pain.
I'd show the world what
It would be like.
To live like me for the
Rest of their life.

Philip Reay
Ryton Comprehensive School

WITHOUT A HOME

He sits there cold, he has no fixed abode,
He drinks his way through day and day.

Cold crushes,
Will anyone notice him?

The sea of people pass,
A uniform rouses him from thoughts of
Gnawing hunger,
The comfort of warmth.

He makes ends meet,
By selling magazines on the street.

He's a down-and-out alone throughout.

John Bolland (14)
Ryton Comprehensive School

WITHOUT A HOME

It was not my fault, I say to myself.
That I'm on my own, without a home.
They could have tried to keep me there,
I don't think that they even care if I live
or if I die.

I remember that day, oh so well.
It was a cold and frosty winter's day.
The trees shook and the wind blew,
Then all of a sudden, it all became true.

I was on my own, cold and helpless,
Nowhere to go, no friends to turn to.
I could never go back, no never to them.
They treated me like a piece of dirt.
I'll never see nor hear them again.

Never a thought, not even a whisper.
Nothing to show that they care or wonder.
They didn't try, they didn't search.
So many questions, no one to ask.

Now what do I do, where do I go,
Where should I run to, now I'm alone.
Who do I turn to, the hostels, the police, the streets.
I'm on my own, no money, no life.

Hayley Ford (14)
Ryton Comprehensive School

THE OWL

His eyes are as big and round as oranges,
His nose pointed like a pin,
His ears loose and wavy,
His feathers are strong and beautiful,
So detailed, as if carefully painted on.
His chest, white and fluffy,
But claws are sharp and could kill in a dig,
His mouth loves chewing mice, crunch, crunch.
The owl is a night-bird,
Swooping low then grabbing his poor prey,
His job done, for the night,
So he sleeps in the day.
Sleep well, night-bird.

Danielle Davidson (11)
St Edmund Campion RC School

WONDERFUL WHALE

This wonderful whale,
So big, but so gentle,
She glides through the water like a snake on
the sand,
As she searches for food,
The sounds that she makes, can be heard
for miles,
She swims with her young,
Keeping them from danger,
She moves to the surface,
Ducking in and out of the water.
This wonderful creature.
This wonderful whale.

Lauraine Bell (11)
St Edmund Campion RC School

DOGS AND CATS

Everyone stared at this dog,
The biggest dog in town,
His eyes were like rocks,
With fur like bristles,
His ears hung far, far down.

As the coolest cat,
Walked down the street,
He was tapping his small, tiny feet,
The cat was:
A small cat (of course),
A brown cat,
A green-eyed cat,
A purrrfect cat,
His eyes were like emeralds,
His ears were like a soft, silk cloth,
Rubbed against my skin.

Kate Lambton (11)
St Edmund Campion RC School

SNAKE

The snake slithers slowly like a snail,
He is green and brown, with slimy scales,
He hisses madly, across the sand,
And leaves his mark upon the ground,
As he wanders along the dry land,
Looking for a mate,
People gaze in surprise,
To see a snake pass before their eyes.

Annmarie Castlehow (11)
St Edmund Campion RC School

BULLYING

They stand by the hall
staring at me looking -
Here they come.
I try to run but I can't.
Something is holding me back.

Then I realise it's one of them
I feel sick with fear.

The biggest boy lifts up his arm
high into the air,
clenches his fist and then,
Down it comes.
          Bang!

It makes contact.
I fall to the floor
and hit my head.
I am clean out.
          Knocked out.

I feel sick with terror.
I don't want to step out of
my back door.
Everywhere I go,
To school or even my backyard.
I feel they're watching me.
Ready to jump out on me
and hurt me.

Liam Hurst (11)
St Edmund Campion RC School

WHY?

I stand around the field gates,
Wondering what will happen next.
I stand there crying,
Feeling the pain of my horse, dying.
I hear a cry from the yard,
It sounds like he's dying,
Why is my horse dying?

He's lying there behind the stable gate.
I wonder, is he dead?
I looked at him one more time,
To see how weak he was.
Then I stepped away.
I heard from a far distance, 'He's dead,'
That's all I heard in my head.
I looked, one more time.
I kissed him, then said 'Goodbye.'
Why is my horse dying?

I looked once more,
He raised his head,
As I shouted, 'Yes, he's not dead!'

Natalie Candlish (11)
St Edmund Campion RC School

THE SPIDER

It's coming to the corner with strength and agility,
Its rhythm is so steady, just like the military,
Its home is black,
It's in a crack,
I've seen it there before,
I wouldn't like to go there and knock upon its door.

He's coming towards me with very puzzled eyes,
He must think if he kills me, he'll win a big, big prize,
He's walking very slow,
He stoops very low,
He's gonna pull my legs off one by one, all eight,
When all I want to be, is his little black mate.

Thomas McTaggart (12)
St Edmund Campion RC School

THE TRUTH BEHIND THE SNAKE

S inuous snake slithering on the sand
N asty, noisy, naughty, nosy
A snake is really not that bad
K inky, curly, twirly, snakes
E xotic ones are colourful
S o beautiful, better than God can make

A snake is not slimy or wet
R eally believe it or not
E ven humongous pythons make great pets

N ot only are they quiet and neat
O nce you get to know them
T hey won't need walking along the street

S nakes put you to the test
C anaries and hamsters, they like the best
A small one, a big one, bigger than you
R eally they're not scary
Y es! It's true!

Rachel Hurst (12)
St Edmund Campion RC School

THE SEASIDE

Hear the seagulls squeal, shout and screech
as they plummet down to the beach.

The fishermen pass by
under a dark, dull, thundery sky.

Suddenly the waves come up and lash
and then come down with a thundering crash.

The lighthouse brightens up the dark night
reaching out to sea, bearing bright light.

Christopher Archibald (11)
St Edmund Campion RC School

MY MONSTER

My monster has 6 eyes
My friend's has only 2
My friend's can skip
Mine can do flips
Mine has 3 lanky legs
His has, just the 1
My friend's eats nothing
When mine eats a ton
Mine has green and purple spots
His has red and yellow
He says his is the best
I say mine's a green ghastly ghoul
Mine can jump and land with a thud
His can wave his arms and sing
After all that arguing
Mine was the real McCoy
Because his was just a toy.

Robert Devlin (11)
St Edmund Campion RC School

JAYNE

You're the petal on a flower
That smells like heaven
Your hair is like a sheet
of black skin

You're the sun
at dawn
the friend that talks when I am *sad*
the sweet smell in the morning

You're the silent one in class
the girl who smiles all the time
You're a cloud
floating in the air

You're a kitten
in some wood
You're my very
Best Friend.

Kimberley Greenup (11)
St Edmund Campion RC School

THE KING OF THE JUNGLE

He sleekly sleeps all through the day,
he roams the jungle at night.
He slowly crawls up to his scrumptious meal,
Pounces! Then bites.
He's hard as a rock and really vicious,
The monkeys swing away as he licks
his lips and says 'Um they look delicious.'
I wonder who's going to be next?

Jenna Marchbanks (11)
St Edmund Campion RC School

BEHIND NEXT DOOR'S FENCE!

Behind next-door's 12 foot fence
There's a scraping crawling sound
But no one will climb up there
And have a look around.

They're frightened they'll get pulled over
Like poor old Katie Brown
Who didn't stand a chance
When the creature pulled her down.

Katie was a little girl
Skinny, pale and shy
One night she heard a frightening noise
And started to scream and cry.

Katie decided to go to the garden
To see what was going on
Then she decided to climb the fence
And *Po boom* she was gone

Now 12 months later
Katie's still not around
So no one dares to climb the fence
Because the creature's ready to pound.

But the mystery's still unsolved
For what the creature is doing there
Marching the yard like an army or two
But ha! We're moving this year.

Adele McDonald (11)
St Edmund Campion RC School

A GREMLIN

A gremlin came from above
his eyes dark as death
he wandered round for quite some time
then called his master Seth.

He had a mask on his face
and a cape from head to feet
he had a tail made of steel
and moved in a beat.

His arms are long and green
his feet are very thin,
he had a brain made of chips
one arm of tin.

He is a dark black blur
and a creepy figure,
he touches you on your neck
which really makes you shiver.

Kieran Taylor (11)
St Edmund Campion RC School

MY CAT

My cat is grey and soft.
With white paws and sharp claws.
His purr sends you mad
It really bugs my dad.
He scratches my wallpaper.
My mam goes mad.
She says she'll get rid of him.
We are all sad.

Louise Hindmarch (11)
St Edmund Campion RC School

THE MYSTERY CREATURE

I was walking in the park,
On my way home,
When I heard a rustling sound,
I saw it move swiftly,
It moved so quickly,
I never saw what it was.

I was in my house,
When I heard a clatter,
I ran outside but there was nothing there,
A bear, a racoon it could have been anything,
But what?
Scratching, scraping it had to be it,
It sounded like the scratching of nails on a desk,
I went outside, it was there,
A tortoiseshell cat.

Sarah Lawson (11)
St Edmund Campion RC School

MY DOG

My dog's a sly dog,
But she'll always be my dog,
When you take her for a walk,
It's as if she can talk,
She'll sit on the ground,
That means it's homeward bound.

When it's time to eat,
She sits at my feet,
To see what there is to eat,
She eats the lot.

Alan Hetherington (12)
St Edmund Campion RC School

BILLY THE WONDER FISH

Even as a child he was
efficient and fast.
Gliding through the water like a
ship at full mast.

He'd win all races, tournaments
and prizes.
He'd win medals and trophies
of various sizes.

He roamed the oceans
and the seven seas.
Protecting the little fish
which puts them at their ease.

When the Fish Princess was
out swimming one day.
Along came a sea hagg
and took her away.

So Billy was called to the rescue
and rescue he did that.
He killed that wicked sea-hagg
and took the princess back.

When Billy returned home
the king was delighted.
He set a celebration
and Billy was duly knighted.

Katie Diston (12)
St Edmund Campion RC School

THE GOLFER

The golfer is short and fat,
Huffing and puffing as he walks along.
He fiddles with the clubs like I don't
Know what,
Trying to choose the right one.

He tees up a ball and takes a practise swing,
His swing is as smooth as a sheet of silk.
Suddenly *Bang!* As he strikes the ball,
Then the ball lands on the green and stops dead.

As he walks to the green, feeling really proud,
Plop, it drops in the hole.
As he picks it out
He noticed it's cracked.

He runs into the clubhouse,
Shouting and bawling.
Everyone is amazed at the sight,
Wow they all said.

In the house alone,
In a frame, stands that ball.
Every time he goes back to the course,
He tries to repeat the same thing.

Christopher Brigham (11)
St Edmund Campion RC School

THE DINOSAUR NEXT DOOR

A dinosaur, a dinosaur, a dinosaur, next-door
with razor teeth,
a vicious roar,
it's the dinosaur next-door

With beady eyes,
a vicious smile.
If you see him you'll run a mile.
It's the dinosaur next-door.

I'm warning you, don't go near him!

Nathan Cartwright (11)
St Edmund Campion RC School

TO MY HANDSOME YOUNG FELLOW

You're the love of my life,
I always think of you in everything I do.
You can be so stubborn at times,
But can be so kind.

Your hair is so blonde and so fine,
Your fingernails are like white lumps of sugar,
Your ears are so so red.

You're like a cute fluffy rabbit,
Your lips are so soft,
Your eyes are so blue.

I haven't seen you for one hour,
And I can't put up with it.
I can barely sleep at nights,
When I can sleep you're in all of my dreams.
You come and save me when I'm in danger,
So will you come run away with me,
And we can be together forever.

Diane Morris (14)
St Edmund Campion RC School

I WISH I HAD A DOG

I really wish I had a dog,
I'd play with him for hours,
Running in and out the house,
And go outside to play.

I wish I had a little dog,
That was as white as snow,
A lovely, little, fluffy dog,
That likes to go for walks.

I really wish I had a dog,
That wouldn't scratch or bite,
It wouldn't bark, it wouldn't whine,
And wouldn't run away.

Lindsey Burn (11)
St Edmund Campion RC School

JADE (MY COUSIN)

You're as loud as a herd of elephants
You're as mischievous as a few monkeys.

You're as old as your grandad
You are an everlasting battery.

You are like a supermarket, storing food
You are like a clown making people laugh.

You're the icing on the cake
You are a fox always on the alert.

Steven Bolton (11)
St Edmund Campion RC School

Rachel (My Best Friend)

You're a crazy puppy, when you want to play.
You're a bouncy ball, when it just goes on bouncing.
Your skin is like the petal of a rose.

You're kind and gentle, like a teddy bear,
Your voice is like an elephant, playing in the grass,
You're the sunshine on a daisy.

You're a branch on a tree, so different,
You're like a moon's reflection off a river,
You're like a sun that always has a smile.

You're a monkey playing around,
You're like a tape that never stops,
You're a rainbow in the sky.

Lucy McGinley (11)
St Edmund Campion RC School

Princess Diana

She will always be the woman in our heart.
She helped everyone that was ill.
She is the bubble that will never pop.

She's the brightest blossom on every tree.
She'll always be the sun drifting across her land.
She is the first cold tear-drop from someone's eye.

You will always be the teddy on my bed.
You will always be the flower in my garden.

I hope someone continues her work.

Cheryl Dorosz (11)
St Edmund Campion RC School

IN THE CUPBOARD

In the cupboard it's dark and damp
something watching me night and day
big green eyes watching me
what it is, I can't say

At night I'm still, as can be
because I know it's there
watching me, even stalking me
it could be a man or even a bear

It could have teeth like razors
I haven't got a clue
my mam says, it is a load of nonsense
but to me it's true.

Shona Richardson (11)
St Edmund Campion RC School

SENSIBLE SNAKES

Sensible snakes, all soft and shiny
What a pity silly people think you're slimy.
Forked-shaped tongue, flicking out to smell
your prey.
It's enough to send some humans grey.
Beautiful and graceful
As you see him wind from side to side.
When people see him, they want to hide.

Laura Dines (11)
St Edmund Campion RC School

SOREYA

Tomorrow I'll miss you just like today,
I love you and miss you so much
I can't explain,
Your words were so soft innocent
and sweet,
For you my love grows each
and every day.

Your big brown eyes like
big saucers,
Your soft tanned skin was
like a feather across my hand,
Your sparkling smile gave me hope,
Every morning you were bright and
cheerful, just like a summer day.

To see you lying there without
any pain brought happiness
but also sadness, to my heart.

Ashya Jacobs (13)
St Edmund Campion RC School

JEFFREY (MY BROTHER)

You're the bear with the giant claw.
You're the poison in the python's fangs.
You're the violence in a lion's roar.
You're the luckiness in a lucky bag.
You're the Menace in Dennis.
You're the fun in my computer.
You're the man on the moon.
You're the freshness in the air.
You're my brother.

David Powell (11)
St Edmund Campion RC School

MY MAM

You're a sunflower,
blowing in the wind,
your skin shines in the sun,
golden tan on your skin,
soft as a hamster's fur.

You're as bright as the sun,
going through the sky,
you're cream, whipped so smooth.

Your eyes are dull like mist,
but they sparkle in the sky,
you roar like lion, *rrroooarrr!*

You're talking so quietly to monkeys,
a rainbow sparkling in the sky,
you're the moment,
I like.

Alison Fish (11)
St Edmund Campion RC School

DONNA (MY SISTER)

You are a lovely rose
blossoming in the summer.
You are the lightning in a thunderstorm.
You are the snap as the crocodile
eats its prey.
You are the breeze on a hot
summer's day.

Jamie Gribbin (11)
St Edmund Campion RC School

ANDREW (MY FRIEND)

He's like a violence in the hurricane
He's the moment of the drip hitting the sink
He's the darkness in a black sun and the light of the world

He's as funny as a laughing clown
He's the sting in the scorpion's tail
He's the buzz in the bees
He's the violence in the tiger's roar

He's the fizz in the can of pop
He's the sweetness of the sugar
He's as dark as a cave
He's the wetness of the morning dew

He's the roughness of the wind and the softness of the breeze
He's the rattle in the rattlesnake's tail
He's the glisten on the spider's web.

Christopher Harding (11)
St Edmund Campion RC School

THE LOVE OF MY LIFE

When I wake up in the morning I always think of you.
Your hair is so smooth like the feel of silk,
Your eyes are so bright they glow in the night,
And when I see you I go all red.
You are like the smell of daisies in the spring.
We are like Romeo and Juliet deeply in love.
Your voice is so soft like a baby's first word.
At every moment I always think of you.
Your hair is the colour of golden straw,
And when I go to bed I know I'll dream of you.

Craig Fielding (13)
St Edmund Campion RC School

DANIELLE BURNS (MY FRIEND)

You're as tall as a lamppost,
You're as silly as Mr Bean,
You're the monkey in our games,
The one who makes us laugh.

You're like a puppy
That plays all day,
And you're a flower
Because you're nice.

You're like a star
That twinkles so bright,
You're like a tub of ice-cream
To keep me happy all day and . . .

You smell like a sweet smelly rose
That's just opened,
You're as fast as a racing car
But sometimes you can be slow,
You can be a pain,
For instance a stitch in my side after running.

You're like the sand sliding through my toes,
Your a kind of Diana because you're my friend,
You're my very best friend to me, a very good friend.

Theresa Atkinson (11)
St Edmund Campion RC School

MARY MCGILL

I am worried as can be
About my friend's mother sobbing on her knee.
Her face looks sad and lonely and
I wish I could only . . .

She's drowning her sorrow with fags and booze.
I try to help but there's nothing I can do.
I feel like I am helping but I haven't got a clue . . .

I am so worried I feel sick.
There's nothing I can do so I feel thick.
I try to help as much as I can,
But I fall on my face again and again.

Robert Crabtree (13)
St Edmund Campion RC School

MY SISTER

You are the snow that falls at day
A bat that flies at night
Your skin is like a silk dressing-gown
Your eyes are bluer than the sea.

Your voice sounds like a squeaky mouse
That's running upstairs
You are a cat that plays gently
With other children.

You're the sunflower that grows
Tall and straight in the wind
You run like an athlete
At the end of a race.

Malcolm Hurst (13)
St Edmund Campion RC School

Puppy Business (About My Dog)

When you were young I hugged and kissed you,
You were cute and cuddly like a teddy bear.
When you bit at my socks and got told off,
I didn't mean to tap your nose.

When you slept all day and grunted like a pig,
I felt like hugging you and not leaving go.
Your little yap which is supposed to be a bark,
Would not frighten a baby.
When you chewed my hair and licked my face,
I was not sure if you loved me or not.

When you were older and mated going to have pups,
You had an infection, you had an operation.
I knew I'd see you through.

Danielle Munn (11)
St Edmund Campion RC School

Danielle (Friend)

You're the friend who is always there,
You're the girl that is brighter than the sun.

You're the creak of the door,
You're the eagle that glides through the sky,
You're the bang of the big loud drums.

You're the slithery snake that sneaks around,
You're my shadow that is always there,
When the sun is out.

You are like the soft clouds in the sky,
You are the kind face I see every day.

Marie Kanu (11)
St Edmund Campion RC School

THE MAGIC BOX

I will put in my box . . .

A thirteenth hour on a clock
1000 tongue tanglers
A day without a night

I will put in my box . . .

One metre of silk thread
The sound of the calm sea
100 sunflowers as bright as gold

I will put in my box . . .

A segment of the juiciest orange
1000 unanswered questions
The darkest night and the brightest day
Ten howling wolves

I will put in my box . . .

Spring bursting in and new life being born
The silver moon and the frozen air

I will put colour in my box . . .

Black a mystical black as the universe
And printed on my box there will be

Keep out it's my magic box!

Amber Bone (11)
St Edmund Campion RC School

LYNDA (MUM)

You're like the rose that blooms all year round,
The special friend that never goes far,
The beautiful butterfly drifting from flower to flower,
And the ink that's in my pen.

You are the determination that runs through me,
And the water in my glass.
You are the stars in the sky and
The strength that is in me.

You're like the wind blowing through my hair,
And the bright coloured flower that shines in the sun.

You are a budgie that tweet, tweets all day long,
You're like the clouds floating in the sky.

Kelly McKee (11)
St Edmund Campion RC School

WEATHER

The moon and the stars both come out at night
The blazing sun and the clouds are now gone
Nightfall has come and all is in darkness
Everyone's sleeping until it is light.

Light comes it's raining and no one's outside
Water drips from every white cloud as rain
The sun comes out and dries up all the rain
The sky turns bright blue and the flowers bloom.

The sun turns to snow and the day is cold
The white snowflakes from the sky above
The snow is so cold it turns your cheeks red
When the sun comes out the white snow will melt.

Samantha Johnson (13)
St Edmund Campion RC School

Magic Box

I will put in my box:

The sparkling stars from the sky above,
The sleet and the snow from off the ground,
The wind and the breeze from the midnight air.

I will put in my box:

A big large elephant,
A tiny little mouse,
The blood from a monkey,
The moo from a cow.

I will put in my box:

The spotless ship from the sparkling sea,
The crackling engine from the bus passing by,
The magnificent plane from the deep blue sky,
The huge rusty train from the long shiny track.

I will put in my box:

The weird worries from the wondering world,
The shocking swords and the gutless guns,
The big long aches and the terrifying pains.

These are the things I wonder about
When I'm sitting alone with nowhere to go,
I wonder why God made all these things
For me to put in a box and lock them away.

Cheryl Duggan (13)
St Edmund Campion RC School

BEN (MY FRIEND)

You're a jackal when you start to laugh,
The one that always surprises someone.
You're the one that's not quite there yet,
The one that's wondering what to do.

You're the brains of a stegosaurus,
The one that stands out from the crowd.
You're the Leaning Tower of Pisa,
Ready to fall at any minute.

You're an aeroplane going nowhere,
You always forget what you've just done.

You're always doing something new,
You are never left out.
You're lucky,
You are Ben.

Joseph Jackson (11)
St Edmund Campion RC School

MARK

You're the prick in a thorn,
You're the sting from a bee,
You're like the wind in the trees,
You're a sneaky fox on skis.
Your hair is like a wave
With surfers at a rave.
You're like a wolf howling on the hills;
You're like the mice which a cat kills.

Ryan Quinn (13)
St Edmund Campion RC School

LIAM ROBSON (FRIEND'S BROTHER)

He is as squeaky as a mouse
And as skinny as a rake,
He's as silly as a clown.

He is as small as an ant,
He's as soft as a pillow.
He can be funny sometimes.

He's as light as a feather floating down.
He has brown eyes like the bark on a tree
And he's always playing football.

He's as sly as a fox
And as loud as an elephant's footsteps,
And when he sings he sounds like a girl.

He's the hyena with the funny laugh.
He's the moaning in my ear.
He's the one who makes me laugh.

Victoria Dornan (11)
St Edmund Campion RC School

LOVE LIVES

I love he,
He loves me,
We shall sit beside
The sand and sea.
We will love each other forever,
We will always be together.
He's the centre of my heart,
I loved him from the start.
So we will never fall apart.

Dawn Foster (13)
St Edmund Campion RC School

Lucy (My Best Friend)

You're the sun that shines through night and day;
You're the smile that never droops;
You're the rabbit that's in the field;
You're the swan that glides elegantly along the water;
You're the girl that stands out in a school photo;
You're the friend that never ends.

You're the light in the darkest corner of the Earth;
You're the one and only sun;
You're the rainbow after the rainstorm;
You're the lion marching round the jungle.

You're the leaves that never change colour;
You're the tea that never ends;
You're the one that never turns away;
You're the sun, moon and all the stars
Shining all around the world.

You're all around at one time;
You're the ink that never runs out;
You are one of a kind.

Eileen Doyle (11)
St Edmund Campion RC School

Batty

B est centre mid-fielder in England.
A ll the teams wanted you.
T hen Newcastle got you.
T he teamwork is good.
Y ou are class in a glass.

David Goundry (13)
St Edmund Campion RC School

My Death

Buried six foot under the ground,
Coffins and corpses all around.
All alone in the middle of the night,
I lie and imagine the grieving above,
From all the people that I love.
As I think I begin to cry,
Why, oh, why did I die?
Was I a bad ungiving person?
I didn't deserve a death this horrific.
The car I was in veered off the road,
That was because of the heavy load.
As the car crashed into the tree,
I could feel the flames dancing over me.
When the paramedics eventually arrived,
I had already died.

Ruth Ashburner (13)
St Edmund Campion RC School

Asprilla

Asprilla is amazing when he's on the ball.
He has got skill like a hawk.
The speed like a cheetah with rubber legs.
The power of his shot.
The height of his crosses.
The joy of his goals.
The excitement when he comes on.
The treasure of his autograph.
The thrill of his free kick.
The glory of his hat trick when he gets it.

Lee McLain (13)
St Edmund Campion RC School

AMY

You're like a candle in the dark,
The smell of just baked bread.
You're like the rainbow after the rain,
A bud in springtime blooming.

Your eyes are like buttons on a clown's suit,
Sapphires sparkling in the sun.
Your smile is like a baby's first word,
A present opened on Christmas day.

You're like the sun coming up at dawn,
The sound of money clanging.
You're like a watch showing the time,
A splash of ice cold water.

Your feet make the footprints in just fallen snow,
The muddy mess at the door.
Your hands do the artwork on walls or on desks,
Having a sister like you wins every contest.

Sarah Lambton (13)
St Edmund Campion RC School

DIANA

There's a pain that hurts so bad
You're the sweetest princess the world's ever had
I feel I know you deep inside my heart
Even though we've been so far apart

Through the gates of Heaven's love
I see you smiling from above
Watching your boys as they grow
Each day they love you more and more

We'll keep your memory deep inside
We'll never forget your joy and pride
Your memory will forever be
Of the sweetest woman inside of me

You left this world in a tragic way
Sunday was such a lonesome day
You'll never be bothered by the press
Goodbye sweet princess, time to rest.

Jill Clark (13)
St Edmund Campion RC School

THE DREAM

You're sitting in the garden in the pitch black,
The wolves begin to howl and the dogs do bark.
Your body begins shuddering in the night's wind.
There is a shadow standing by the gate,
He moves closer, I try to run away.

I begin to panic thinking of my safety,
You can hear his breathing as heavy as a brick.
His deep and sharp hello whispers through my head.
He hits me on the head and knocks me out,
I wake up in my bed it's all a dream.

The sweat is dripping from my rosy cheeks,
I'm breathing very heavy I'm panting like mad.
I look at my clock it's 2am.
You walk to the window to check the gate,
You're wrong he is still there waiting for you.

Amanda Dawson (13)
St Edmund Campion RC School

DIANA

Diana the Queen of Hearts will be remembered forever more,
The silence the flowers the sadness the grief,
The coffin the horses the lilies on top,
The Queen and the family bowed as she passed them all by,
A cry and a shrill from the public, heart-breaking,
The young princes, Charles and her brother adoring,
A hand on their young shoulders to comfort them a touch,
Into the Abbey her body gently carried tears were a'flowing,
The words of the Archbishop remembered her life, God rest her soul,
'Candle in the Wind' the song moved us all,
The words of her brother's voice broken and torn,
Earl Spencer will carry on the upbringing she taught,
We remember you forever, God keep you and love you
Forever and more.

Marie Bryant (13)
St Edmund Campion RC School

LEE

You're the love of my life,
You're the sun in the sky.
The moon and the stars,
And that is no lie.

You're the love of my life,
You're the beat in my heart.
I have always adored you,
Right from the start.

You're the love of my life,
You're the one for me.
I only love you,
It was meant to be.

You're the love of my life,
You're my dream come true.
Together forever,
I'd die without you.

Nicola Robbins (13)
St Edmund Campion RC School

DANCING

Pretty dancers in a row
Judges seeing how they go
Flying through the open floor
People cheering at what they've saw.

Sparkling costumes all around
Blaring music's quite a sound
Results are called you've made it
You don't regret it one small bit.

Pressure's now died down in your head
We can go home and be fed
All year round your made to train
Primrose is near it starts again.

Samantha Johnson (13)
St Edmund Campion RC School

SEASIDE FEELING

I stand on the cliff, majestic and high,
A choir the wind and waves make together.
King Neptune orders the seagulls to sing,
A wonderful harmony rises high.
The wind dances with the breeze on my cheeks,
The scarf I wear pulled tighter to my neck.
People below throw branches for their dogs,
They scurry around catching for their owners.
I slowly walk back, turn to face away.
I turn off the TV *wow!*
What a programme!

Clare Mead (13)
St Edmund Campion RC School

THE CAT

Quietly crawling through the deserted streets,
Padded paws pattering on the ground
And in the moonlight the black cat
Softly scales the wall.

With a tail's swish and claws' scratch
It sits, its silvery silhouette shaking.
The glowing street lamp casts a shadow
And the curious green eyes stare.

It begins to sing a sorrowful song,
Telling us of his life,
But with a mouse's squeak and a dog's bark,
The black cat is gone.

Rachel Ford (15)
St Anne's Mixed High School

THE CAR

I love the car,
I love the car,
I love its graceful ease,
Speeding through winding, country roads;
Whistling past bushes and trees.

I hate the car,
I hate the car,
I hate its putrid smell;
The grey and dirty smog it makes,
Like a vapour cloud from hell.

I love the car,
I love the car,
I love the speed and skill with
Which it travels down the motorways,
Like a hunter after a kill.

I hate the car,
I hate the car,
I pity those it kills
As maniac drivers speed and overtake
Upon the brow of hills.

I love the car,
I love the car,
The Toyota and the Fiat,
The Nissan Primera, Micra, Almera
And the wonderful Seat.

The Rover and the Mini,
The Escort and Sport MG,
Enough of them, but the BMW,
Now that's the car for me!
I really do like the car!

John Smith (12)
St Joseph's RC Comprehensive School

SCRAMBLER

I love the bike
I love the bike
I love the way it revs
I love the way it speeds along
And turning every head.

I hate the bike
I hate the bike
I hate the noise it makes
I hate the way it streaks along
And pulls its squeaky brakes.

I love the bike
I love the bike
I love the way it rolls
I love the way it twists and turns
And wheelies down the road.

I hate the bike
I hate the bike
I hate the fumes it makes
I hate the way it puffs and pants
And dirties every place.

I love KX I love CR and P Wee TY 2
By writing this poem I love the bike
I hope I've made you too.

John McIntyre (13) Daniel Adde & Andrew Richards (12)
St Joseph's RC Comprehensive School

COMPUTERS

I like computers,
I like computers,
I can do my homework.
I like computers,
I like computers,
I am not a berk.
I like computers,
I like computers,
They have great games.
I like computers,
I like computers,
I'm in the hall of fame.

I hate computers,
I hate computers,
They give me square eyes.
I hate computers,
I hate computers,
I think I'm going to cry.
I hate computers,
I hate computers,
How do you switch them off?
I hate computers,
I hate computers,
They're better in the loft.

There's a Playstation, a Saturn and a Mega Drive too,
A N64, but a PC will do.

Karl Murphy & Sean Gray (12)
St Joseph's RC Comprehensive School

THE COMPUTER

I love the computer
I love the computer
I love the way it clicks
I love the computer
I love the computer
Its megahertz and its chips

I hate the computer
I hate the computer
I hate the way it hurts your eyes
I hate the computer
I hate the computer
I hate to say goodbye

I love the computer
I love the computer
Nintendo's 64 bits
I love the computer
I love the computer
And PCs are the number one hit

I hate the computer
I hate the computer
I hate its loading time
I hate the computer
I hate the computer
I couldn't think of anything to rhyme

I love Nintendo
I love Sega
I love Sony and also Amiga
People say it rots the brain
But I love the computer all the same.

Adam McDowell (12)
St Joseph's RC Comprehensive School

THE PLANE

I love the plane,
I love the plane,
Its speed, its height, its stamina.
The way it cruises through the air,
I love the plane.

I hate the plane,
I hate the plane,
The turbulence and the rain.
The way it throws the plane about,
I hate the plane.

I love the plane,
I love the plane,
Waving at the people below.
Seeing all the tiny bodies it's like
The Monopoly show,
I love the plane.

Andrew Brabbs & Dean Lupton (12)
St Joseph's RC Comprehensive School

A PERFECT PLACE

Time in some places is something to crowd things into.
Time can be something that needs to be filled up
And in a perfect place, time goes by,
As I wander in a familiar garden.

Eleanor Earl (11)
Sacred Heart Comprehensive (Lower School)

MY PARADISE

I run, towel under arm, tripping and rolling over
a bright green cow-covered field,
Stumbling eagerly down the dusty brown bank.
There it is! My paradise!
The fast-flowing, bubbling sweet-smelling river.
Quickly, I get changed on the smooth hot rocks
shaded by a drooping tree.
I rush down to the crystal clear river.
It's freezing! - I run up to the bridge
and cross over to the other side.
The sharp jagged rocks are jutting out high above the water.
From the bank I can see a mass of brightly coloured
shimmering rocks all lying at the bottom.
The river looks deep and so cold!
The hot sun beaming down on my back and face relaxes me.
I hear the birds singing and the water rushing beneath me,
As well as the sound of cows mooing gently in the distance.
I take a run back and . . . jump! There is a rush of air
swooshing past me as I fall.
I get an icy cold feeling as I hit the water, with a great splosh.
For a split second I wonder if I will ever rise to the top.
I get a wonderful warm welcoming feeling
as a shaft of sunlight hits my face when I surface.
I reach out to grab something and my fingers feel a large
smooth rock poking out of the water, I hold on and don't let go.
The strong, strong fast current is pulling hard!
My hands slip under water and I swallow some.
It tastes sweet and refreshing.
Gradually I slow down and land by some smooth warm rocks.
I climb out and wrap my towel around me.
I sit down and let the hot sun soak up the water from my skin.

Susie Batey (12)
Sacred Heart Comprehensive (Lower School)

ONE WORD

Stretching fingers across a map,
Each time I see,
One word,
Memories brought back.

A white house by itself,
Bright against haze,
Floating in,
Half-conscious, in a daze.

Numbers on a door,
Still,
Unread, unreadable
Shapes in my head.

Now in flowing motion,
Through many open doors,
The sound of people chatting,
Seeping through the floor.

Outside,
A view,
Of green, and blue,
A faraway town,
Way, way down.

Walking through a fast motion world,
No one to hear one single word.

Alex Reynolds (11)
Sacred Heart Comprehensive (Lower School)

A COUNTRY FARM

Hay cracking underfoot
Scratching my arms as I walk past
The sweet smell of dry hay
Is what I like best.

Blowing gently through my hair
The wind also sways the treetops
The fresh clean air
Is what I like best.

The tractors are buzzing
The stream is gargling
Miles upon miles of patchwork countryside
Is what I like best.

High trees to climb
Their leaves falling thickly in the autumn
The stickiness of the sap from underneath the bark
Is what I like best.

At night it is very quiet
And the stars are very bright
The little rodents are scuttling
The hedgehogs are rustling
But in the house everybody is asleep and soundless
This is what I like best of *all!*

Joanna Cooke (11)
Sacred Heart Comprehensive (Lower School)

LANERCOST

Everything was so peaceful in the cottage.
The only noise we could hear,
Was the soft trickling of the streams nearby
And the joyful song of the birds in the sky.

The warm sun beat down on us,
As we lay on the freshly cut grass,
Watching every movement
Of the animals that passed.

Even now,
Far away from my favourite place,
I can hear the rustling of the leaves,
Moving at a steady pace.

Lara Stewart (11)
Sacred Heart Comprehensive (Lower School)

A WORLD OF SILENCE

The cold shivers up me like the Snow Queen with her wand.
The clouds seem like cotton wool in a little child's picture.
Sharp stones hurt my feet like a hundred shining knives.
I feel as happy as a fairy tale princess.
The heat creeps slowly into me like the sun rising in the morning.
Rustling of the wind moving through the trees
Reminds me of the waves but there's no waves in this lake.
It's a world without sound here.
A world of silence.

Rachael Kain (11)
Sacred Heart Comprehensive (Lower School)

FAVOURITE PLACE

On a summer's midday,
The children and I lie in the sun.
We lie on the bridge, with the water underneath,
In the heat the sprinkler shooting on you,
With the smell of the fresh air it just could not be better.
Looking up at the bright blue sky and
Wondering what the clouds could make.
The slight breeze is unbelievable,
How it runs through your toes like a dozen spiders.
When you've been lying in the sun all day
And quickly dip your toe in it feels like
A wiggly worm wriggling through you body.

Janine Hope (11)
Sacred Heart Comprehensive (Lower School)

MY FAVOURITE PLACE

Horses' hooves clipping and clopping,
Rabbits and hares hoppety hopping.
The sweet smelling air all around,
Daffodils and snowdrops on the ground.
Birds singing in the air,
Woodpeckers pecking on trees everywhere.
Fluffy clouds like cotton balls,
This is my favourite place of all!

Kaye Walton (11)
Sacred Heart Comprehensive (Lower School)

In The Garden

Peace
Relaxation
Sweet smell, you just want to eat some.
Hot air.
The feel of the soft wind blowing.
No one is around but me.
Everything's so still.
The smell of flowers.
You're so relaxed you just feel like
You just want to drop off to sleep.
The sweet sensation.
You're in a lovely dreamy mood.
You think it's just a dream and
You're going to wake up but you're not.
The water's so soft like a towel rubbing on your face.
You just cannot be bothered to move,
You just want to laze around all day.
When you first lay down you thought you weren't going to like it
But when you got used to it, you feel so soft and delicate.

Kelly Martin (11)
Sacred Heart Comprehensive (Lower School)

Breathless

Wind crossing across my face
Running across fields of corn.
Feeling free as a bird
Flying through the air.
My wings spread out wide,
My love of freedom,
Now I can set it free.

Caroline Brown (11)
Sacred Heart Comprehensive (Lower School)

GRANDMA'S HOUSE

Crunching gravel stones under my feet
as I excitedly walk to the door.
Greeted by a smiling Grandma and cousins.

Stepping through the door
The delicious smell of Grandma's dinner meets me,
making my mouth water.

Sitting in the living room,
Listening to Grandma talking about her latest holiday
and how well the tomatoes are doing. Presents all round.

Playing in the garden with my cousins,
I can hear the pots being washed in the kitchen
and the birds singing.

Looking down the garden I can see lots of trees and flowers
and as I walk down the path I see rows and rows of vegetables
that my Grandma has grown and the greenhouse.

Memories of me and my cousin going to feed the ducks
and pushing each other in the old pushchair.
Memories of playing with the old handbag and all the bits and bobs.
Memories of sitting on the coal bunker,
Of trying to find a pen that works
and playing with the playing cards.

This is my Grandma's house all round
What a lovely place to be.

Rachel Kennedy (11)
Sacred Heart Comprehensive (Lower School)

MY FAVOURITE PLACE

Hear the waves crashing against the rocks,
Or the sand rolling down the dunes,
Leaping clouds rolling around in the sky,
You'd love this Heavenly place.
It is full of mystery,
Sound is disguised by stillness,
Life steeped in history,
A small isolated land,
Never ending peace.
Dwells here, in . . .

Nicola Miles (12)
Sacred Heart Comprehensive (Lower School)

CAMPING SITE - MY FAVOURITE PLACE

Peaceful wind blowing through the trees.
Blue cloudless sky, big yellow shining sun.
Freedom, fresh air, tall trees, animals and birds.
Happy, friendly, carefree people walking here and there.
Lots to do and see.
Swimming, walking in the woods, crazy golf,
Climbing trees, bike riding, and barbecues.

It's lots of fun on the campsite.

Hayley Davidson (12)
Sacred Heart Comprehensive (Lower School)

THE WORLD

As I watch the bright sun begin to set,
All I hear is the birds as they tweet.
Looking up into the bright blue sky,
Watching as the birds fly by.
I smell the hay that is so sweet
And see the ponies as they eat.

As I see the sun get brighter,
The children begin to walk to school.
They do not notice as the cool sun is beaming,
Then come the younger children faces gleaming,
With delight they're starting school.

The world is such a delicate place,
Only some people notice.
So many people just forget about the sunset
and other wonderful things,
But some people care I can tell by their face,
All so happy with this place.

Sarah Coulson (13)
Warbottle Campus